INTRODUCING
ISSUES WITH
OPPOSING
VIEWPOINTS®

Commercial Space Exploration

M. M. Eboch, Book Editor

GREENHAVEN
PUBLISHING

Published in 2019 by Greenhaven Publishing, LLC
353 3rd Avenue, Suite 255, New York, NY 10010

Articles in Greenhaven Publishing anthologies are often edited for length to meet page requirements. In addition, original titles of these works are changed to clearly present the main thesis and to explicitly indicate the author's opinion. Every effort is made to ensure that Greenhaven Publishing accurately reflects the original intent of the authors. Every effort has been made to trace the owners of the copyrighted material.

Library of Congress Cataloging-in-Publication Data

Names: Eboch, M. M., editor.
Title: Commercial space exploration / M.M. Eboch, book editor.
Description: New York : Greenhaven Publishing, 2019. | Series: Introducing
  issues with opposing viewpoints | Audience: Grades 7-12. | Includes
  bibliographical references and index.
Identifiers: LCCN 2017058411| ISBN 9781534503595 (library bound) | ISBN
  9781534503601 (pbk.)
Subjects: LCSH: Outer space--Civilian use--Juvenile literature. | Space
  tourism--Juvenile literature. | Space industrialization--Juvenile
  literature.
Classification: LCC TL794.7 .C66 2019 | DDC 338.0999--dc23
LC record available at https://lccn.loc.gov/2017058411

Manufactured in the United States of America

Website: http://greenhavenpublishing.com

Contents

Foreword   5

Introduction   7

Chapter 1: What Is the Future of Space Tourism?

1. Expect Delays in Space Tourism   11
   Jason Davis
2. NASA May Suffer From Political Changes   18
   Casey Dreier
3. Private Space Companies Will Thrive Under
   President Trump   26
   Bryan Bender
4. The Benefits of Private Space Exploration   33
   Lina Shi

Chapter 2: What Are Some Challenges with Commercial Space Travel?

1. Revolutionary Changes in Technology Will Come
   from NASA   40
   Jonathan Coopersmith
2. Space Colonies Can't Solve Humanity's Challenges   47
   Edward Tenner
3. Space Travel Is Full of Potential Dangers   53
   Jessica Boddy
4. Space Law Needs an Update   59
   Anél Ferreira-Snyman
5. The Risks and Rewards of Sending People into Space   65
   Joshua Colwell and Daniel Britt

Chapter 3: Are We Going to the Moon or to Mars?

1. We Can Return to the Moon—to Live   71
   Matt Williams
2. We Can Colonize Mars (Eventually)   79
   Matt Williams
3. NASA Isn't Going to Mars Anytime Soon   87
   Eric Berger

4. It's a Long, Hard Road to Mars   93
   Mia Brown
5. Exploring Space Makes Life on Earth Better   98
   Space Foundation

Facts About Commercial Space Exploration   106
Organizations to Contact   108
For Further Reading   112
Index   115
Picture Credits   119

Foreword

Indulging in a wide spectrum of ideas, beliefs, and perspectives is a critical cornerstone of democracy. After all, it is often debates over differences of opinion, such as whether to legalize abortion, how to treat prisoners, or when to enact the death penalty, that shape our society and drive it forward. Such diversity of thought is frequently regarded as the hallmark of a healthy and civilized culture. As the Reverend Clifford Schutjer of the First Congregational Church in Mansfield, Ohio, declared in a 2001 sermon, "Surrounding oneself with only like-minded people, restricting what we listen to or read only to what we find agreeable is irresponsible. Refusing to entertain doubts once we make up our minds is a subtle but deadly form of arrogance." With this advice in mind, Introducing Issues with Opposing Viewpoints books aim to open readers' minds to the critically divergent views that comprise our world's most important debates.

Introducing Issues with Opposing Viewpoints simplifies for students the enormous and often overwhelming mass of material now available via print and electronic media. Collected in every volume is an array of opinions that captures the essence of a particular controversy or topic. Introducing Issues with Opposing Viewpoints books embody the spirit of nineteenth-century journalist Charles A. Dana's axiom: "Fight for your opinions, but do not believe that they contain the whole truth, or the only truth." Absorbing such contrasting opinions teaches students to analyze the strength of an argument and compare it to its opposition. From this process readers can inform and strengthen their own opinions, or be exposed to new information that will change their minds. Introducing Issues with Opposing Viewpoints is a mosaic of different voices. The authors are statesmen, pundits, academics, journalists, corporations, and ordinary people who have felt compelled to share their experiences and ideas in a public forum. Their words have been collected from newspapers, journals, books, speeches, interviews, and the internet, the fastest growing body of opinionated material in the world.

Introducing Issues with Opposing Viewpoints shares many of the well-known features of its critically acclaimed parent series, Opposing

Viewpoints. The articles allow readers to absorb and compare divergent perspectives. Active reading questions preface each viewpoint, requiring the student to approach the material thoughtfully and carefully. Photographs, charts, and graphs supplement each article. A thorough introduction provides readers with crucial background on an issue. An annotated bibliography points the reader toward articles, books, and websites that contain additional information on the topic. An appendix of organizations to contact contains a wide variety of charities, nonprofit organizations, political groups, and private enterprises that each hold a position on the issue at hand. Finally, a comprehensive index allows readers to locate content quickly and efficiently.

Introducing Issues with Opposing Viewpoints is also significantly different from Opposing Viewpoints. As the series title implies, its presentation will help introduce students to the concept of opposing viewpoints and learn to use this material to aid in critical writing and debate. The series' four-color, accessible format makes the books attractive and inviting to readers of all levels. In addition, each viewpoint has been carefully edited to maximize a reader's understanding of the content. Short but thorough viewpoints capture the essence of an argument. A substantial, thought-provoking essay question placed at the end of each viewpoint asks the student to further investigate the issues raised in the viewpoint, compare and contrast two authors' arguments, or consider how one might go about forming an opinion on the topic at hand. Each viewpoint contains sidebars that include at-a-glance information and handy statistics. A Facts About section located in the back of the book further supplies students with relevant facts and figures.

Following in the tradition of the Opposing Viewpoints series, Greenhaven Publishing continues to provide readers with invaluable exposure to the controversial issues that shape our world. As John Stuart Mill once wrote: "The only way in which a human being can make some approach to knowing the whole of a subject is by hearing what can be said about it by persons of every variety of opinion and studying all modes in which it can be looked at by every character of mind. No wise man ever acquired his wisdom in any mode but this." It is to this principle that Introducing Issues with Opposing Viewpoints books are dedicated.

Introduction

"There are thousands of people who would love the opportunity of becoming astronauts and going into space."
—Richard Branson, founder of Virgin Galactic

Millions of people have dreamed of becoming an astronaut. In 2013, 200,000 people applied to live in a Mars settlement that may be decades away from being a reality. This shows the drive to go beyond the boundaries of our planet.

And yet only twelve people have walked on the moon. Only a few hundred have ever traveled into space. Most people who have reached the Earth's upper atmosphere are professional astronauts. Every time the National Aeronautics and Space Administration (NASA) allows applications, 2000 to 6000 people apply. Usually no more than 10 become astronauts. Meanwhile, just a handful of tourists have gotten as far as the International Space Station orbiting Earth. They paid millions for the privilege.

With so much demand, and so little opportunity, is it any wonder that commercial space travel is a multibillion-dollar dream?

The Soviet Union launched the first person into orbit around the Earth in 1961. The same year, Alan Shepard became the first American to fly into space. President John F. Kennedy gave a speech to Congress requesting support for an increased space program. He said, "I believe that this nation should commit itself to achieving the goal, before this decade is out, of landing a man on the moon and returning him safely to the earth. No single space project in this period will be more impressive to mankind, or more important for the long-range exploration of space; and none will be so difficult or expensive to accomplish."

He was right about the challenge and the cost. But for Kennedy, national pride came from beating the rival Soviets to the moon. After Shepard's success, Kennedy referenced "the impact of this adventure on the minds of men everywhere." He understood the excitement everyone felt about exploring the universe. "[I]t will not be one man going to the moon…," Kennedy said, "it will be an entire nation."

America reached that goal in 1969. On July 20, Astronaut Neil Armstrong stepped onto the moon in what he called a "giant leap for mankind" Six Apollo missions explored the moon between 1969 and 1972. The world had entered the Space Age.

The Space Age did much more than send people into space. Many advances came out of the research and development needed to allow space travel. Fields from aviation to medicine benefited from new technology. Rockets sent communications and navigation satellites into orbit. Television, telephones, and the internet depend on these satellites. So do computers, mapping systems, and weather forecasting. Satellites are used to defend the country, conduct surveillance during wartime, and investigate disasters. The Space Age has brought extraordinary benefits to the general public in many ways.

And yet, today space travel is no more accessible to the average person. A few private space tourists have paid over $20 million each for a ten-day visit to the International Space Station (ISS). Virgin Galactic offers space tours for $200,000 per person. These go only 60 miles up, far below Earth's orbit. A person has not stepped on the moon since 1972. Mars is still a distant dream.

NASA has changed its priorities for space exploration for a number of reasons. Because NASA is dependent on federal funding, its budget can change from year to year. The agency is hesitant to commit to expensive long-term programs that may be cut before they are completed. Safety is also a priority for NASA. In 2003, the space shuttle *Columbia* disintegrated as it returned to Earth. Seven crewmembers died. In addition, debris fell to earth. Although no one was injured by the debris, it pointed out a potential danger to the general public. This led to the decision to discontinue the Space Shuttle Program after the ISS was completed.

NASA continues to send astronauts to the ISS to do research, via Russian spacecraft. NASA also sends spacecraft farther into space, but without crews. Probes and robotic devices send back photos, maps, and other information, teaching us more about our solar system. NASA plans to send humans to an asteroid by 2025 and to Mars in the 2030s. However, some people doubt the organization's ability to accomplish this.

Meanwhile, several private companies are pursuing spaceflight. Their focus is on the commercial potential, the ability to make a profit. Income could come from charging tourists for spaceflights. One goal is to lower the cost of spaceflight so it is more accessible to ordinary people. Other commercial opportunities include carrying NASA astronauts for a fee, and mining minerals in space. One private company, SpaceX, says its goal is "to revolutionize space technology, with the ultimate goal of enabling people to live on other planets." Founder Elon Musk claims SpaceX could send humans to Mars by 2024. He envisions a settlement of a million people by the 2060s. That would mean not only taking people to another planet, but finding a way to supply all they need to survive for years.

Such endeavors face extreme technical challenges and can cost millions or billions of dollars. To date, most space programs, whether government-funded or private, miss most of the deadlines they set for themselves. The challenges of sending people into orbit, let alone to the moon or to Mars, are extreme. But as Kennedy said, "We choose to go to the moon in this decade and do the other things, not because they are easy, but because they are hard."

Does the future of space travel lie with NASA or with private companies? Will space travel ever become cheap and easy? Will we get to Mars in a few years, a few decades, or never? The current debates about commercial space travel are explored in Introducing Issues with *Opposing Viewpoints: Commercial Space Exploration*, shedding light on this ongoing contemporary issue.

Chapter 1

What Is the Future of Space Tourism?

Will we soon be flying to outer space on spring break?

Expect Delays in Space Tourism

Jason Davis

> *"[SpaceX] have made incredible leaps forward in technology while re-energizing the world about spaceflight in a way that NASA has failed to do."*

In the following viewpoint Jason Davis examines the likelihood that SpaceX will send space tourists around the moon in 2018. SpaceX, or Space Exploration Technologies Corp., is a private company that manufactures and launches rockets and spacecraft. SpaceX claimed in early 2017 that its new rocket would be ready for a flight with a crew by the end of 2018. The author notes that SpaceX, like other private space companies and the government agency NASA, has often missed deadlines. Davis predicts that SpaceX may do what they claim—but probably not when they say it will happen. Davis is a journalist for The Planetary Society, an organization supporting space science and exploration.

AS YOU READ, CONSIDER THE FOLLOWING QUESTIONS:

1. How long would the space tourism flight around the moon last, according to the article?
2. What is the Joint Confidence Level used by NASA?
3. By how much does SpaceX typically miss its deadlines, according to the author?

"SpaceX plans to send tourists around the Moon in 2018. Here's why that may not happen," by Jason Davis, The Planetary Society, March 3, 2017. Reprinted by permission.

On Monday, SpaceX announced plans to send two space tourists around the Moon next year. The audacious, week-long flight would take place using a Falcon Heavy rocket and Crew Dragon spacecraft and be the first time humans have been beyond low-Earth orbit since 1972.

Some media outlets have compared the mission to *Apollo 8*, humanity's first crewed mission to lunar space, which happened in 1968. In terms of traveling to a vantage point where Earth is a small blue-and-white orb dangling in darkness of space, that's certainly true. *Apollo 8*, however, slowed down and entered orbit, whereas the Crew Dragon would use a "free-return" trajectory, whipping around the far side of the Moon to slingshot back toward Earth.

A more accurate mission comparison, therefore, is *Apollo 13*.

After an oxygen tank explosion crippled the spacecraft of Jim Lovell, John Swigert and Fred Haise during a trip to the Moon in 1970, NASA had to abort the mission. Unfortunately, it's practically impossible to turn around when you're halfway between the Earth and the Moon, traveling 11 kilometers per second; the only option is to use the free-return maneuver.

It's hard to say whether these two SpaceX customers could work themselves out of an *Apollo 13*-esque crisis. They have asked not to be identified; all we can really say about them is that they must have a lot of money. SpaceX isn't saying how much the duo will pay for tickets, but some available cost comparisons include the amount tourists have paid to fly on Russian rockets (at least $20 million), the average cost of a SpaceX or Boeing seat to ship an astronaut to the ISS ($58 million, according to one report), and the amount NASA currently pays Russia for Soyuz seats ($80 million).

Risk and price tag aside, what are the chances SpaceX can actually pull off this bold mission in 2018?

Not good—and here's why.

A Quick Analysis of Past Announcements Shows SpaceX Misses Major Milestones By About 2 Years.

SpaceX is well-known for its ambitious timelines. To be fair, they're in good company on this front: many spaceflight firms, and also NASA,

Space X's Falcon 9 rocket lifted off in 2016 with an unmanned Dragon cargo craft. SpaceX has lofty goals but has not met its proposed timeline.

are similarly guilty of underestimating how long major projects will take. That's why NASA's science programs—and more recently, its human spaceflight programs—use a metric called the Joint Confidence Level, or JCL, to calculate the odds something will be delivered on time based on available funding levels. In short, NASA doesn't commit to a launch date until a JCL analysis says there's a 70 percent chance it will hold.

I went through SpaceX's past press releases and official statements to see if I could quantify the average delay time for major milestones. I found that on average, SpaceX misses publicly stated deadlines by an average of 2.1 years.

Some well-known examples of these delays include the first crewed Dragon flight (originally promised in 2014, but yet to occur) and the Falcon Heavy (originally promised for 2013 or 2014, but yet to launch). Again, to be fair, an analysis of other NewSpace companies or NASA would likely turn up similar results. But that doesn't make it any less true.

The GAO Thinks SpaceX May Not Be Certified For ISS Crew Rotation Flights Until 2019.

On February 16, the Government Accountability Office released a report saying SpaceX and Boeing might not be certified to fly ISS crews until 2019.

Before NASA signs off on SpaceX for astronaut transportation, the company must conduct two demo flights of its new Crew Dragon spacecraft. The first will be an uncrewed test flight, which SpaceX expects to occur in November. The second will take place with two astronauts, and SpaceX says the mission will be ready to fly in May 2018.

The GAO is skeptical of those dates. Among the reasons: SpaceX plans to make two more upgrades to the Falcon 9 this year, before showing NASA the rocket's design is finalized and stable—prior to the November uncrewed test flight. There's also an ongoing debate about the company's plan to fuel the rocket with astronauts aboard, and questions about the significance and mitigation of cracks found in Falcon 9 engine turbines.

SpaceX Preisdent Gwynne Shotwell recently told reporters at Kennedy Space Center she was confident the first crew flight would occur in 2018. If that happens in May as scheduled, NASA certification could come between July and September, followed by the first official ISS crew rotation flight.

Where, exactly, the Moon tourist mission would fit in to that schedule is unclear, considering the company has a backlog of other missions to fly after last year's launch pad explosion. In theory, SpaceX could proceed with the flight anytime—it's just a question of whether they are potentially willing to risk looking bad in the context of their NASA partnership.

Flying tourists after the first paid ISS crew rotation flight would seem to be the most prudent; NASA has been without the capability to launch its own astronauts since the space shuttle retired in 2011. The agency made a big bet on commercial crew providers after canceling the Constellation program in 2010. As of last year, NASA still provides the bulk of SpaceX's revenue, and in Monday's announcement, SpaceX went out of its way to thank the agency for shouldering most of the development cost of Crew Dragon.

NASA, meanwhile, has been forced to lay the groundwork for using Russian rockets to reach the ISS in 2019 (ironically, the seats are being purchased through Boeing) in the event SpaceX and Boeing crew flights are delayed further.

The Current Record For Introducing a New Launch Vehicle and Subsequently Using It to Fly Humans to the Moon Is 13 Months. SpaceX Has About 18.

The Crew Dragon tourist flight requires the Falcon Heavy, which is expected to make its first test flight this summer. That gives SpaceX a maximum of 18 months to hit its 2018 deadline.

The Falcon Heavy will be the most powerful rocket operating since the Saturn V, which debuted during *Apollo 4* in November

1967. That flight sent an uncrewed Apollo capsule to an altitude of 17,300 kilometers, causing it to slam back into the atmosphere at 11.1 kilometers per second, putting the capsule's heat shield through the same stresses it would encounter upon returning from the Moon. In December 1968, 13 months later, the first crewed Saturn V flight sent *Apollo 8* to lunar orbit.

Unlike *Apollo 8*, SpaceX's tourists won't need the capability to slow down and enter lunar orbit, and then speed up again to come home—so that simplifies things. But it also doesn't sound like SpaceX is planning to make a high-velocity Crew Dragon test flight. By the end of 2018, the spacecraft may have returned from low-Earth orbit a couple times, but those reentries will have been slower—about 7.7 kilometers per second.

All In All, There Are A Lot of Unanswered Questions, and SpaceX Isn't Providing More Details.

The first hint of this announcement came on Sunday, Feb. 26, when SpaceX CEO Elon Musk tweeted "SpaceX announcement tomorrow at 1pm PST." On Monday, 1:00 p.m. came and went, and at about 1:25, a flood of tweets from various media outlets broke the Moon mission news. SpaceX released a brief written statement a few minutes later. It was soon revealed that a select group of reporters had been invited to attend a press teleconference with Musk. The call was apparently brief, lasting less than a half hour.

It's not uncommon for organizations, both private and public, to control the flow of information by preferring certain media outlets over others. NASA, however, makes their briefings publicly available—even though not everyone gets a chance to ask questions, everyone gets to hear what others are asking. Additionally, NASA public affairs officers generally work with reporters to answer followup questions (even if the answers turn out to be non-answers).

I sent an email to SpaceX about all this, asking if they'd consider inviting more reporters to their briefings—even with less-preferred outlets in a listen-only mode—or whether they had an audio recording of the most recent teleconference, or whether they'd be willing to answer a few written questions about the Moon mission.

The answer was no.

Which brings me back to the premise of this article: Based solely on publicly available facts, it seems unlikely this mission will happen in 2018.

Objectively speaking, SpaceX has revolutionized the launch industry. They have made incredible leaps forward in technology while re-energizing the world about spaceflight in a way that NASA has, in some ways, failed to do. They broke the monopoly on launching classified US payloads. They may one day send humans to Mars.

For a space company that has only been around for 15 years, that's extraordinarily impressive. But in terms of media relations and gut-checking ambitious timelines, there's always room for improvement.

EVALUATING THE AUTHOR'S ARGUMENTS:

In this viewpoint, Jason Davis expresses skepticism that Space X will meet its stated goal for sending people to the moon. He claims that it is difficult to get accurate information from SpaceX, so he looked at their past delays. Is studying a company's past history a good way to judge their future successes? Why or why not?

NASA May Suffer From Political Changes

Casey Dreier

"We just don't know how planetary science will fare."

In the following viewpoint, written just after Donald J. Trump was elected president, Casey Dreier predicts how the new administration is likely to affect NASA. Dreier notes likely cuts to NASA's Earth science programs, which include the study of climate change, and the cancellation of the Asteroid Redirect Mission, which was designed to closely study an asteroid. He expects planetary study to continue, possibly along with progress toward human spaceflight to either Mars or the moon. However, large cuts in overall government funding could make it difficult for NASA to continue with many missions. Dreier is Director of Space Policy at The Planetary Society, a nonprofit foundation.

AS YOU READ, CONSIDER THE FOLLOWING QUESTIONS:

1. What three areas of focus are typical of a Republican candidate, according to the article?
2. Is NASA more likely to send people to Mars or the moon, according to this viewpoint?
3. What is the biggest challenge to NASA's future funding, according to the article?

"NASA Under Trump," by Casey Dreier, The Planetary Society, November 18, 2016. Reprinted by permission.

NASA's ongoing missions are always at risk when a new administration takes over.

With the election of Donald Trump as the 45th President of the United States, space policy experts and fans alike are trying to grasp the implications for NASA. In the past week, many people have written solid analyses of likely near-term changes. However, the real problem is that there are not much data to work with. At this point, everything is going to be speculation to some degree.

I want to provide some additional detail to this existing analysis, particularly by looking at the bigger picture budgetary forces that may be buffeting NASA over next four years.

What We Know

Before the election, advisers working with the Trump campaign released two op-eds late in the campaign that outlined the candidate's broad space policy agenda. The campaign also provided answers to questions submitted by SpaceNews and ScienceDebate regarding space. The answers and op-eds were general, outlining broad ambitions and stating positive platitudes about the space program. This lack of detail is not unusual for presidential campaigns. But the broad outlines were relatively standard for a Republican candidate: a focus on human spaceflight, deep space exploration, and public-private partnerships. A skeptical eye was cast on Earth science and the duplicate efforts underway to build heavy-lift launch vehicles. Trump himself said that he would "free" NASA from being a low-Earth orbit logistics agency, echoing statements in the published op-eds.

However, we have learned that Robert Walker, who co-wrote the space op-eds for the Trump campaign, has no role on the transition team, and is likely ineligible to serve in the Administration at all since he is a registered lobbyist. It is unclear, to say the least, what this means for the space policy ideas laid out in those op-eds (the other co-author, Peter Navarro, is an economist and not a space policy expert).

One of the concrete proposals in the campaign statements was to reconstitute the National Space Council, which has historically coordinated and defined US space policy under leadership of the Vice President. This idea has received support from the Chair of the House Space Subcommittee. But note that a National Space Council is not in itself a statement of policy—it is effectively a plan to make a plan.

Additional clues can be mined by paying close attention to the staffing choices made by the Trump Administration and his transition team. It has been reported that Mark Albrecht will lead the transition for NASA. Albrecht is a solid and experienced choice who served as the executive secretary for the George H. W. Bush Administration's National Space Council and has worked in the space industry for decades (to get a sense of his perspective and experience, you can read his book, *Falling Back to Earth*).

Beyond that, we have no confirmed staff on the transition team related to civil space. NASA has not yet been contacted by Trump's team. A NASA Administrator likely won't be appointed, much less confirmed by the Senate, for many months. There are already several names that are publicly associated with the job, but don't pay too much credence to those just yet. As the old DC saying goes, "those who know aren't talking and those who are talking don't know".

Now let's look at some specific topics that will certainly be relevant during the next year of transition and the new Administration.

Earth Science

The fate of Earth science at NASA is almost certain to be the most controversial issue facing the space community in the next few years. The division will lose its privileged funding position under a Trump Administration (of all the sciences, it alone has enjoyed consistent growth of its budget under Obama). We don't know exactly what sort of cuts to expect, or even if there will be an attempt to remove Earth science from NASA's portfolio completely. But previous statements by members of the congressional Republican majorities, as well as Trump himself, likely guarantee some decrease in funding.

Adding to this uncertainty is that Earth science lost two senior, well-positioned Democrats that have defended it in the past: Mike Honda in the House and Barbara Mikulski in the Senate, both of whom served as ranking member (e.g. top-level) Democrats on their respective Commerce, Justice, and Science (CJS) appropriation subcommittees that write NASA's annual funding bills. While both were replaced by other Democrats, these new members of Congress will lack the seniority enjoyed by Honda and Mikulski, and may not even serve on the same committee. It remains to be seen which Democrats will serve as the new ranking members on these committees, and what level of attention they will apply to NASA.

Planetary Science

I include this section only because of our members' interest and focus in this science. We just don't know how planetary science will fare. It was not mentioned directly, though it seems to fit in with the broad goals of exploring deep space. John Culberson (R-TX) will return to Congress as the Chair of the critical CJS subcommittee on appropriations, and he will continue to prioritize NASA's mission to Europa and (hopefully) Mars exploration and planetary science in general.

#JourneyToMars

NASA is currently on a #JourneyToMars, but the big question is if this journey will survive a new transition. Many Republican space policy experts believe that the Moon is a more promising destination, which could bode poorly for NASA's Mars ambitions. However, if the Space Launch System rocket and Orion survive into the new administration (and I think they will, since their political support in Congress is very strong), NASA could pivot to the Moon without significant disruption.

However, Mars remains a compelling goal that has the support of major industry partners, SpaceX, and is currently experiencing a high amount of public excitement with movies like *The Martian* and National Geographic's new *MARS* series. If the goal of the Trump space policy is for "human exploration of our entire solar system by the end of this century," then walking away from Mars doesn't make a lot of sense.

Regardless, the general attitude from the President-elect has been a repeated commitment for deep space exploration. That's a positive sign, and either the Moon or Mars would represent an important step for human spaceflight.

Just keep in mind that, at the moment, anything about NASA's human spaceflight goals (including my own paragraphs above!) are pure conjecture. We should have a better idea over the next few months as staffing and policy goals firm up.

Oh, and the Asteroid Redirect Mission? I predict this mission is almost certainly over, given the House's proposal to zero out its budget in 2017 and the Senate's very skeptical stance in recent legislation. Not to mention a general desire of the Trump team to break with Obama Administration priorities.

The Space Launch System and Orion

NASA's largest and most controversial programs are its Space Launch System (SLS) rocket and Orion multi-purpose crew vehicle. Maligned by many but beloved by Congress, these programs were conceived in the wake of the last Presidential transition that cancelled NASA's Moon-focused Constellation program. While the Trump campaign's op-ed on space had oblique references to the SLS in its critique of replicated efforts to design launch vehicles, the basic political case behind the SLS/Orion programs remains as strong as it did in 2010.

For evidence, we can look toward the NASA Transition Authorization Act of 2016, a bipartisan Senate bill which has not yet passed into law. It lays down the overall vision for near-term civil space priorities, one of which is the continuation of SLS/Orion and the focus on deep space exploration. The bill was sponsored by Ted Cruz (R-TX), and co-sponsored by Marco Rubio (R-FL), and Bill Nelson (D-FL), among others. Cruz and Nelson are the Chair and Ranking Member, respectively, on the Senate's science committee. Additionally, the SLS program has enjoyed ongoing support from Richard Shelby (R-AL) who chairs the Senate's CJS appropriations subcommittee. The House also has demonstrated strong bipartisan support for the SLS/Orion programs as well.

This isn't to say that the SLS/Orion programs are impossible to cancel—they aren't. But so far as we know, both of them are still reasonably on budget and schedule for a late 2018 launch. Many of the politicians who wrote those programs into law are still serving in Congress, and a bipartisan bill has been introduced in the Senate that clarifies ongoing support for them. If the Trump Administration wanted to cancel these programs, they would be picking a fight with Congress. Do they want to expend that energy and political capital on this issue? My guess is that they will want to save that for bigger issues that are closer to the new President's primary agenda.

The Budgetary Big Picture Looks Grim

With the exception of Earth Science, I'm not fundamentally worried about the direction of NASA over the next four-to-eight years given what we know so far. NASA still benefits from being generally non-partisan, and the individuals we've seen associated with the transition and potential Administration are competent, committed people.

But this doesn't necessarily mean NASA is in for an easy future. Despite good intentions, there are some serious headwinds that could buffet the space program given the larger political and monetary implications of Trump's and congressional Republicans' agendas.

Let's look at what we know. The Trump campaign's tax cut plan would reduce government revenues by $4.4 trillion to $5.7 trillion over the next ten years. In addition, he has proposed a $1 trillion infrastructure plan over the same time period. Combined, those would place enormous monetary pressure on the rest of government.

The US government's annual budget is approximately $4 trillion, but Congress actively appropriates only about a quarter of that—approximately $1.2 trillion—every year. The other $3 trillion is spent automatically, mainly for social safety net programs. Congressional Republicans have already signaled their intent to cut these expenditures under a Trump Administration to an unknown extent.

Of the $1 trillion of "discretionary" spending, more than half is spent on national defense. Everything else the government does—scientific research, border control, education, environmental protection, federal judges, infrastructure, NASA—comes from this non-defense discretionary amount. This has also been targeted for wholesale cuts by the Trump campaign in order to help pay for their large tax cut. These cuts, along with the reinstitution of the sequester (across-the-board cuts to all federal agencies), would collapse non-defense discretionary spending to its lowest point in modern history.

This budgetary scenario potentially spells doom for NASA and its ambitions. The congressional subcommittee responsible for NASA—Commerce, Justice, and Science—is also responsible for the NSF, NOAA, the FBI, the Justice Department, and Commerce Department, and the Census, among others. This committee receives a fixed allotment of money from the congressional budget committees, and then have to use that amount to fund all of their agencies. If the overall amount of discretionary spending falls, then the CJS subcommittee will likely receive a smaller allocation, and they will have less money available to fund NASA and every other agency within their purview (particularly given the fact that they prioritize basic needs: paying judges, feeding prisoners in the federal penitentiaries, national security programs within the FBI, and so forth). Adding to the mix, the Census, one of the few constitutionally-mandated expenditures in government, will also be ramping up in its funding needs over the next four years, adding even more competition for this limited funding.

With the exception of the Apollo era, NASA's budgetary increases and decreases have generally tracked the overall amount of discretionary spending. So even with strong Congressional support, NASA would struggle greatly to maintain its current portfolio of missions. It's just math.

Again, this scenario depends on decisions that have not yet been made, and actions not yet taken. It will depend on the size of the tax cut and infrastructure plan, and how much effort is made to pay for it. But the point remains: regardless of rhetoric, if the promised tax cuts and spending cuts come to pass, the next four years will be tough terrain for merely maintaining NASA's current slate of programs, much less expanding them beyond Earth.

EVALUATING THE AUTHOR'S ARGUMENTS:

In this viewpoint, Casey Dreier looks at the challenges NASA faces when it comes to receiving funding from the US government. Should NASA be subject to changes in funding based on who is president and who is in Congress? Why or why not?

Private Space Companies Will Thrive Under President Trump

Bryan Bender

"No NASA program dominated by bureaucrats could take the risks, accept the failures and create a learning curve comparable to an entrepreneurial approach."

In the following viewpoint, Bryan Bender examines the Trump administration's goals for exploring space. This article was written nearly 3 months after the previous viewpoint, a few weeks after Trump took office. Therefore, Bender had more specific information about the Trump administration's goals. He notes a focus on the economic development of space. This would prioritize programs designed to earn money rather than research for the sake of science. NASA would focus on supporting private companies and on exploring deep space. Much of the space program would be privatized, or switched from governmental control to private ownership. Bender is a journalist and the defense editor for Politico, a journalism company that covers politics and policy.

"Trump advisers' space plan: To moon, Mars and beyond," by Bryan Bender, Politico LLC., Februrary 9, 2017. Reprinted by permission.

AS YOU READ, CONSIDER THE FOLLOWING QUESTIONS:
1. What are "Old Space" and "New Space," as described in the article?
2. When might private spaceships circle the moon, according to Trump's transition team mentioned in the article?
3. What space activities would *not* be given to the private sector, according to the article?

The Trump administration is considering a bold and controversial vision for the US space program that calls for a "rapid and affordable" return to the moon by 2020, the construction of privately operated space stations and the redirection of NASA's mission to "the large-scale economic development of space," according to internal documents obtained by POLITICO.

The proposed strategy, whose potential for igniting a new industry appeals to Trump's business background and job-creation pledges, is influencing the White House's search for leaders to run the space agency. And it is setting off a struggle for supremacy between traditional aerospace contractors and the tech billionaires who have put big money into private space ventures.

"It is a big fight," said former Republican Rep. Robert Walker of Pennsylvania, who drafted the Trump campaign's space policy and remains involved in the deliberations. "There are billions of dollars at stake. It has come to a head now when it has become clear to the space community that the real innovative work is being done outside of NASA."

Old and New Space

The early indications are that private rocket firms like Elon Musk's SpaceX and Jeff Bezos' Blue Origin and their supporters have a clear upper hand in what Trump's transition advisers portrayed as a race between "Old Space" and "New Space," according to emails among key players inside the administration. Trump has met with Bezos and Musk, while tech investor Peter Thiel, a close confidant, has lobbied

President Donald Trump has emphasized the economic potential of space. In 2017 he signed an executive order to reestablish the National Space Council.

the president to look at using NASA to help grow the private space industry.

Charles Miller, a former NASA official who served on Trump's NASA transition team after running a commercial space cargo firm, is pushing for the White House to nominate a deputy administrator who foremost "shares the same goal/overall vision of transforming NASA by leveraging commercial space partnerships," according to a Jan. 23 communication. That deputy would run the space program's day-to-day operations.

Trump has yet to name a NASA director, but the documents confirm that Rep. Jim Bridenstine, a Republican from Oklahoma and former Navy pilot who ran the Tulsa Air and Space Museum, is a top contender.

"Fingers crossed," Miller writes of Bridenstine's candidacy, according to one email.

The White House and Miller did not respond to requests for comment.

Former House Speaker Newt Gingrich, another commercial space evangelist with close ties to Trump, is also pushing the White

House to embark on a major effort to privatize US space efforts.

"A good part of the Trump administration would like a lot more aggressive, risk-taking, competitive entrepreneurial approach to space," Gingrich said in an interview. "A smaller but still powerful faction represents Boeing and the expensive old contractors who have soaked up money with minimum results.

"No NASA program dominated by bureaucrats could take the risks, accept the failures and create a learning curve comparable to an entrepreneurial approach," he added. "Just think of the Wright brothers' 500 failures in five summers at $1 per failure. Ask how long NASA would have taken and how much it would have cost."

The more ambitious administration vision could include new moon landings that "see private American astronauts, on private space ships, circling the Moon by 2020; and private lunar landers staking out de facto 'property rights' for American on the Moon, by 2020 as well," according to a summary of an "agency action plan" that the transition drew up for NASA late last month.

Such missions would be selected through an "internal competition" between what the summary calls Old Space, or NASA's traditional contractors, and New Space characterized by SpaceX and Blue Origin.

But the summary also suggests a strong predilection toward New Space. "We have to be seen giving 'Old Space' a fair and balanced shot at proving they are better and cheaper than commercial," it says.

Low-Earth Orbit

Another thrust of the new space effort would be to privatize low-Earth orbit, where most satellites and the International Space Station operate—or a "seamless low-risk transition from government-owned and operated stations to privately-owned and operated stations."

"This may be the biggest and most public privatization effort America has ever conducted," it says.

Granting most of low-Earth orbit activities to the private sector—key exceptions would be made for military and intelligence satellites—is a major element of what Walker, who chaired the House Science Committee, has been pushing Trump to adopt.

Unlike deep space exploration, which under the proposed vision would remain a key element of the government's space mission, in low-Earth orbit "you have mature enough technologies—private space stations in orbit, a number of concepts for building constellations of satellites that would have earth-bound applications," said Walker, who says he now consults mostly for New Space clients.

But he said the potential for economic development there—from space tourism to a host of industrial purposes to include the manufacture of pharmaceuticals and new materials—cannot be fully tapped "as long as the investors think they might be competing with the government."

"Turn over low-Earth orbit to commercial interests," Walker advises. "NASA—your job is to go to deep space. Get back into the business of technology developments that move us more aggressively into the exploration role again," such as a mission to Mars. "You can't do missions of that enormity with chemical rockets."

The proposals being considered by the new administration also call for a "space industrialization initiative" in which NASA, with its $19 billion annual budget, would be "refocused on the large-scale economic development of space," according to the summary.

NASA's Future

The model for NASA's new role, it says, could be the National Advisory Committee for Aeronautics, a federal agency established in 1915, at the dawn of aviation, to promote and institutionalize aeronautical research.

"NASA's new strategy will prioritize economic growth and the organic creation of new industries and private sector jobs, over 'exploration' and other esoteric activities," according to the summary of the NASA agency action plan. "Done correctly, this could create a trillion-dollar per year space economy, dominated by America."

But such an approach is likely to cause anxiety within NASA and in Congress.

"Clearly there is a very keen interest in bringing in commercial but there is still a lot of desire to maintain programmatic continuity," said Andy Aldrin, director of the Buzz Aldrin Space Institute at the Florida Institute of Technology. "At some point those two things may not be consistent. At the end of the day there is only so much money to go around."

At NASA itself, major components of the agency that are focused on human space flight, space science and aeronautics might see their budgets cut or redirected under the new administration. "The uncertainty is not good for the workforce," said Brendan Curry, vice president of Washington operations for the Space Foundation, an educational organization whose members include a wide variety of space firms.

"The sooner that we know whatever the plan is from the Trump administration then Congress can adjudicate on it and the space industry will move ahead," Curry said.

Indeed, the bigger fight over the soul of the space agency could play out on Capitol Hill. Convincing skeptical lawmakers that are worried about the loss of NASA contractor jobs in their districts could be difficult—not to mention finding the additional federal money that might be needed to partner with private space companies.

Lori Garver, who served as the deputy NASA administrator in the Obama administration, predicts major pushback from Congress despite the potentially significant economic benefits of an aggressive government role in the privatization of space.

"We had a new administration that wanted to go in that direction but we were slowed," she said in an interview. "We made a little bit of progress."

While there is a strong argument that privatization would bring new jobs, "they don't want to let it go because they can't ensure where the jobs will be," said Garver, now general manager of the Air Line Pilots Association.

A bitter foretaste of the potential space war was the feud between Space X and the United Launch Alliance—a joint venture between Lockheed Martin and Boeing—over lucrative contracts to launch military satellites into orbit.

Powerful backers of Boeing, such as Sens. Richard Shelby of Alabama and Dick Durbin of Illinois, faced off against SpaceX supporters like Arizona Sen. John McCain, and SpaceX ultimately won a court battle to elbow its way into the military market.

For Aldrin, whose father Buzz was the second human to walk on the moon, the government space effort is a crossroad. He believes that private investment in space will not only bring economic benefits but could help NASA reignite its human space program, which has stalled since the retirement of the space shuttle fleet in 2011.

"We can leverage more investment in commercial markets to provide a better foundation for what NASA would like to do with human exploration," he said. "We have to understand what the relationship between those two things can be. Sound market economics can be a real strong foundation to launching a mission to Mars and human habitation to Mars."

EVALUATING THE AUTHOR'S ARGUMENTS:

In this viewpoint, Bryan Bender addresses the goals of government-funded space programs versus private spaceflight companies. What are some ways the two groups could work together? What are some challenges for each of them individually, and for all working together?

The Benefits of Private Space Exploration

Lina Shi

"The space industry is especially full of opportunities, both for its natural resources and tourism."

In the following viewpoint, Lina Shi argues that there are potential benefits to private space exploration. These include reducing costs for NASA and developing new technologies more quickly. Private companies could also earn money by charging people for space travel, and by collecting minerals in space. These sources of funding could support the companies and allow them to make further advances. However, Shi notes that many private space exploration companies fail to deliver on their promises. They also tend to be focused on commercial applications rather than scientific knowledge. For these reasons, government agencies such as NASA may still have a role to play. Shi is a student at the University of Pennsylvania Wharton School. This article was written for a student blog at the Penn Wharton Public Policy Initiative's website.

AS YOU READ, CONSIDER THE FOLLOWING QUESTIONS:

1. When was private space travel legalized, as mentioned in the article?
2. How has the budget for NASA changed since 1966?
3. How much is one asteroid worth?

"The Implications of the Privatization of Space Exploration," by Lina Shi, Lina Shi, December 12, 2016. Reprinted by permission.

E ver since the legalization of privatized space travel in 2004, more and more companies have been joining in on a new space race.[1] In recent years, companies such as SpaceX and Virgin Galactic have been taking a more active role in space travel. For example, some companies now bring cargo to the International Space Station through private space shuttles and mine precious metals from asteroids.[2] Here we discuss the implications of the privatization of space exploration.

Background

The dream of space exploration has existed throughout human history. Like many other scientific breakthroughs in the US, the capability of space exploration came as a result of military research and development. The merits of long-distance rockets as weapons were realized during World War II, which led to the founding of missile programs by both the United States and the Soviet Union. Throughout the Cold War, the space race continued with each country outdoing the other in space exploration progress, from *Sputnik* to the Apollo moon landings.[3]

However, as the Cold War (and the threat of communism) waned and the fall of the Soviet Union appeared inevitable, the American public became less interested in exploring the cosmos. Since 1993, the budget for NASA has never totaled over 1% of the overall federal budget, in contrast to the whopping 4.41% share of the federal budget it had in 1966. While NASA spent around $44 billion 2015 dollars at the height of the space race, in recent years the agency has received less than half of that amount around $18 billion dollars for its annual budget.[4]

Especially in the modern world of divisive politics in which budgeting priorities are heavily debated, NASA and government funded space exploration have been deprioritized. Since spending for space exploration has not kept up with inflation, major budget cuts have caused many of NASA's programs to shut down. For example, the Space Shuttle program, which brought astronauts and important cargo pieces to the International Space Station, was discontinued in 2011 due to NASA budget cuts.[5]

Some argue that privatization of space travel allows NASA to use its funding for other important areas of research.

To fill the void left by discontinued NASA programs, many private companies have received commissions from NASA to perform important functions. For instance, in place of the Space Shuttle program, NASA has formed Commercial Resupply Services contracts with commercial space companies SpaceX and Orbital ATK to deliver cargo to resupply the International Space Station.[6] While American astronauts currently have to borrow a ride from the Russian vehicle Soyuz to reach the ISS[7], NASA is working on the Commercial Crew Program in conjunction with SpaceX and Boeing to develop spacecraft that can carry astronauts to low-Earth orbit and the ISS.[8]

Benefits

The biggest cited benefit of the privatization of space travel is its cost-effectiveness. For example, whereas the old Space Shuttle program cost around $4 billion each year, the new commercial resupply services contracts only cost around $50 million per launch.[9] Thus,

NASA now has more money available to spend in other areas. Instead of being bogged down by the routine application of old research, NASA can prioritize their limited budget to work more on research of other unknowns and development of new long-term space travel technologies. Additionally, with many private companies all developing new space technologies, there is more competition for innovation, which may also lead to faster growth in the field of space technology.[10]

Proponents of privatized space travel also point out that the private sector often transforms government developed technologies into lucrative or affordable technologies and products for the general public. The space industry is especially full of opportunities, both for its natural resources and tourism. On the natural resources side, precious metals, minerals, and energy are available in infinite supply in space. For instance, one average half-kilometer S-type asteroid is worth more than $20 trillion dollars.[9] Multiple companies have started low-Earth orbit technology to allow people to be launched into space for a short trip. For example, Virgin Galactic famously offers short flights into space for $250,000 dollars.[11] Although the current price is cost prohibitive, limiting this service's potential market, private companies have time to develop government technologies to be more cost-effective in the future. Altogether, these private space exploration companies will take advantage of the opportunities to push existing technology to create jobs and boost the economy.

Costs

Although there are many benefits to privatization, critics are quick to point out that this is an overly optimistic picture. In reality, many private space exploration companies overpromise and underdeliver. In the industry, there have been myriad cases of failed public-private partnerships. For instance, NASA's partnership with Lockheed Martin for an X-33 space shuttle design cost NASA $912 million and Lockheed Martin $357 million.[12]

Additionally, while companies are often able to implement decisions and fund projects faster than NASA, they also have to deal with different competing interests.[13] While NASA has to answer to the interests of the government and taxpayers, private companies have to take into account profitability, the interests of a variety of shareholders, and reliance on a secure contract with NASA. Since profitability is a major factor in a lot of decision making, programs that focus on the general development of space exploration and knowledge, but lack immediate commercial applications, may not be developed. This suggests that there is still a place for the government in space exploration research and development.

Conclusion

Although there are pros and cons to privatizing space exploration, current trends suggest that many of NASA's space exploration responsibilities are being shifted towards the private sector under government contracts. Through private-public partnerships, the United States moves into its next era of exploring the cosmos. Whether this new model will produce discoveries and innovation in-step with former government run space research is yet to be seen.

Endnotes

1. https://www.faa.gov/about/office_org/headquarters_offices/ast/media/PL108-492.pdf
2. https://www.nasa.gov/sites/default/files/files/NASA_Partnership_Report _LR_20140429.pdf
3. https://www.nasa.gov/50th/timeline.html
4. https://www.whitehouse.gov/omb/budget/Historicals
5. https://www.nasa.gov/mission_pages/shuttle/flyout/index.html
6. https://www.nasa.gov/mission_pages/station/structure/launch/overview.html
7. https://www.nasa.gov/audience/forstudents/k-4/stories/nasa-knows/what-is-the-soyuz -spacecraft-k-4
8.https://www.nasa.gov/content/commercial-crew-overview
9. http://www.wsj.com/articles/SB10001424052748703382904575059350409331536
10. http://www.theatlantic.com/technology/archive/2010/02/the-pros-and-cons-of -privatized-space-exploration/346657
11. http://www.virgingalactic.com/human-spaceflight/fly-with-us
12. http://www.wsj.com/articles /SB10001424052748703382904575059263418508030
13. http://www.gcsp.ch/News-Knowledge/Global-insight/The-Privatization-of-Space -When-Things-Go-Wrong

EVALUATING THE AUTHOR'S ARGUMENTS:

In this viewpoint, Lina Shi notes some benefits to private space exploration but suggests that the government still has a role. Are both governmental space agencies and private companies important to the future of space exploration? Why or why not?

Chapter 2

What Are Some Challenges with Commercial Space Travel?

There is a lot to be worked out before space tourism becomes a regular part of our lives.

Revolutionary Changes in Technology Will Come from NASA

"Space travel will not become affordable until the age of rocketry is replaced by an age of new propulsion technology."

Jonathan Coopersmith

In the following viewpoint, Jonathan Coopersmith looks at the technology for launching rockets into space and argues that chemical rockets are outdated, and new technology is needed. With current rockets, much of the weight comes from fuel and expendable rocket stages. The latter help launch the cargo but are then dropped and never recovered. Coopersmith claims that a ground-based system would be better. In this variation, the launch system stays on the ground. The payload, such as cargo and passengers, would travel into space. While a ground-based system would ultimately be safer and much cheaper, it will take billions of dollars of investment over many years. Coopersmith says only the government has the resources to make this commitment. Coopersmith is an associate professor of history at Texas A&M University.

Reprinted with permission from ISSUES IN SCIENCE AND TECHNOLOGY, Coopersmith, "Affordable Access to Space," Fall 2012, p. 57-62, by the University of Texas at Dallas, Richardson, TX.

AS YOU READ, CONSIDER THE FOLLOWING QUESTIONS:
1. What is the biggest factor preventing the large-scale exploration of space, according to the author?
2. How much of a rocket's weight is fuel and expendable rocket parts that are thrown away after one use?
3. What is the difference between a rocket and a ground-based launch system?

R ockets are 20th-century technology. A government effort to develop new launch technologies could open the door to a vast array of new opportunities for space exploration and development.

The high cost of reaching orbit is the major factor preventing the large-scale exploration and exploitation of space. When I fly from College Station, Texas, to almost anywhere in the United States, I pay $4 to $8 per kilogram (kg) of me. When a satellite is launched into space, the customer (or taxpayer) pays approximately $10,000 to $20,000/kg. Space travel will not become affordable until the age of rocketry is replaced by an age of new propulsion technology—and only government action will make that happen.

Since *Sputnik* inaugurated the space age in 1957, chemical rockets have propelled every payload into orbit and beyond. Rockets work well, but they are expensive. Their high costs have restricted access to space to the governments, corporations, and organizations that can afford tens or hundreds of millions of dollars to launch a satellite. Consequently, half a century after *Sputnik*, only a few hundred tons of payloads, the equivalent of two Boeing 747 freighter flights, reach orbit annually. The number of people who have reached orbit since Yuri Gagarin in 1961 could fit into one Airbus 380.

Nor are rockets fully reliable. Their failure rate while carrying communications satellites to geosynchronous orbit in 1997–2006 was 8%. Taurus booster failures in 2009 and 2011 cost NASA $700 million in lost satellites. Insuring a communications satellite from launch through its first year of operation costs 11 to 20% of the total cost, which is two orders of magnitude greater than for a Boeing 747.

Rocket technology has remained largely unchanged since the early days of the space program.

For $125 million, an Atlas V will lift 9,000 kg to low Earth orbit for $14,000/kg, which is much less than the $25 million for the 1,300 kg carried by a Taurus at $19,000/kg. Future developments promise some improvement, but even reducing costs by an order of magnitude, a goal not envisioned by rocket advocates in the next decades, still means a dauntingly high cost. The much-heralded Virgin Galactic space tours cost $200,000 per person (approximately $2,000/kg) but will go only 60 miles up, far below Earth orbit and demanding an order of magnitude less energy.

Under current trends, the technology for reaching orbit in 2030 and beyond will be essentially unchanged from 1957. This continued dependence on rockets is not for lack of effort. Since the introduction of the space shuttle in 1981, the National Aeronautics and Space Administration (NASA) alone has spent over $21 billion on cancelled rocket programs such as the X-33. The military also has its share of cancelled projects, such as the Rapid-Access Small-Cargo Affordable Launch (RASCAL).

Efforts by private firms to develop rockets over the past two decades have largely floundered or become dependent on government funding. The problem is not incompetence or ineptness of governments, corporations, or individuals (although overly optimistic statements have created unrealistic expectations), but the very challenge of leaving Earth. The phrase "It's not rocket science" is part of popular culture for a reason. The technology of designing, building, and launching a rocket into a harsh, unforgiving environment is very demanding.

Why, if the cost and reliability of rockets limit space exploitation and exploration, have alternatives not been developed? First, rockets fulfill existing limited demand sufficiently well to deter the development of alternatives. Indeed, the entire space industry revolves around chemical rockets. The situation is analogous to airplane engine technology in the 1930s, when the efficiency and output of piston engines increased even as their theoretical limits were becoming increasingly apparent. The military demands of World War II and the Cold War greatly hastened the development of the jet engine. No such pressing urgency exists today for rockets.

Second, proposed alternatives to rockets are technologically immature. Moving from the laboratory to practical application will demand billions of dollars over many years. The perceived benefits are too distant for industry or nonprofits to invest serious resources. Only the federal government can provide the sustained commitment over many years that is necessary for development.

And Now for Something Completely Different

The goal is not to develop new technologies for technology's sake, but to develop technologies to drastically decrease the cost of reaching orbit.

One reason why rockets cost so much is that over 90% of a rocket's weight is fuel and expendable rocket stages. The actual payload is only a few percent. The alternative to the rocket is a ground-based system (GBS), which keeps the engine and most of the fuel on the ground, so the spacecraft is almost all payload, not propellant. As well as being more efficient, GBS is inherently safer than rockets, because the capsules will not carry liquid fuels and their complex equipment, eliminating the danger of an explosion.

As with any technology in its formative phase, a range of possibilities exists. Leading contenders include beamed energy propulsion and space elevators. Magnetic levitation and light gas guns have less potential. Most important, the alternatives have the potential to reduce the cost per kilogram by up to two orders of magnitude to $200/kg.

In beamed energy propulsion, a microwave or laser beam from the ground station strikes the bottom of the capsule. The resultant heat compresses and explodes the air or solid fuel there, providing lift and guidance. Researchers in the United States and Japan have propelled small models by lasers and microwaves, demonstrating proof of the concept.

Space elevators employ a thin tether attached to a satellite serving as a counterbalance tens of thousands of kilometers above Earth. A platform holding the payload crawls up the tether. Generating more publicity and better art than beamed energy, this concept depends on the development of materials strong and light enough to serve as the tether.

Magnetic levitation and magnetic propulsion systems would give a high initial velocity to a spaceplane, which would then use a scramjet or rocket to propel itself into orbit. These are not true GBSs, but ways to replace the lower stages of a rocket with a more efficient, less costly way of reaching the upper atmosphere.

The idea of employing a gigantic gun to launch space capsules received a very public unveiling from Jules Verne in his 1865 *From the Earth to the Moon*. Serious development occurred a century later when the US and Canadian governments funded the High Altitude Research Project (HARP) by Gerald Bull in the 1960s and the Super High Altitude Research Project (SHARP) at Lawrence Livermore Laboratory in the 1980s and 1990s. Instead of igniting a conventional propellant, the gun compressed a low–molecular-weight gas such as hydrogen to produce a higher velocity. The small projected payload of only 1 kg helped lead to the project's cancellation. Growing interest in picosatellites, which weigh less than 1 kg, however, may revive interest in very small payloads.

A Game Changer

The concept of GBS encompasses a range of technologies with payloads ranging from a kilogram to hundreds or thousands of kilograms. All assume a high frequency of launches, so that a GBS system could launch thousands of tons per year, an order of magnitude more than current launchers.

[...]

Roadmap to Space

If GBS is such a good idea, why has it not been developed? The good news is that researchers have demonstrated that GBS concepts are theoretically feasible; the bad news is that these concepts remain in the laboratory. On the nine-stage Technology Readiness Level (TRL) scale that NASA and the military use to judge the maturity of a technology, GBS technologies are at TRL 1 or 2, still in the early stages of proving their practicality and worth. GBS faces the classic technological chicken-and-egg conundrum: Demand is too low to justify developing new technologies to reach orbit, because the conventional cost of reaching orbit is so high that it depresses demand. This cycle can only be broken by government action.

For GBS to evolve into a mature, functioning system will require a sustained commitment of billions of dollars over many years. Developing GBS is a legitimate and necessary role of the federal government. Historically, the federal government has supported the development, construction, and operation of transportation infrastructure, including roads, canals, railroads, airways, and highways. Most pertinent, by 1957 the US military had spent more than $12 billion (over $90 billion in current dollars) developing rockets. Without government funding in the 1950s, there would have been no NASA space program in the 1960s.

Rocket development received government funding because of the understandable market failure of the private sector and non-profit organizations. In the 1920s and 1930s, individuals and private groups in Europe and the United States tried building their own rockets. They quickly discovered that rockets demand a commitment of financial, scientific, technical, and human resources far beyond what they could muster. Only a government could provide those resources. Since the 1930s, every country that has developed rockets had the state play the major role in funding and guiding those efforts, whether civilian or military.

[…]

Developing GBS will be expensive, but the failure to create low-cost access to orbit will be even more expensive by delaying the large-scale exploration and exploitation of space. As with nuclear fusion research, the potential is great. Unlike fusion research, the time to success will be much shorter—if the effort is made. Just as government funding developed the technology that enabled humanity's first footsteps into space, so too can the government development of GBS make the second half-century of the space age even more exciting than the first.

EVALUATING THE AUTHOR'S ARGUMENTS:

In this viewpoint, Jonathan Coopersmith suggests that new technology could reduce the cost of spaceflight. However, he notes reasons why that is not happening. Does it make more sense to focus money and effort on current technology, or on developing new technologies?

Space Colonies Can't Solve Humanity's Challenges

Edward Tenner

"We do not now have the technology or experience to explore Mars safely and sustainably."

In the following viewpoint, Edward Tenner explores the possibility of establishing human colonies in space. He notes that it is very hard to predict the future of technology. However, in his view and that of many experts, large-scale space colonies are unlikely. They would be very expensive and technologically difficult to build and maintain. In addition, astronauts would face known and unknown health risks living in space. In the author's view, even if we are able to overcome these problems, we would be better off spending that money and energy improving life on Earth. Tenner is the author of several books and articles, many about technology throughout history.

AS YOU READ, CONSIDER THE FOLLOWING QUESTIONS:
1. What is the risk of death for an astronaut?
2. What are some health risks to astronauts, according to the article?
3. How does the cost of spaceflight affect the likelihood of people colonizing other planets?

"No Exit: Why Space Colonies Can't Solve Humanity's Challenges," by Edward Tenner, American Enterprise Institute, October 24, 2014. Reprinted by permission.

Stephen Hawking, Newt Gingrich, Elon Musk, and Jeff Bezos have at least one thing in common: enthusiasm for large-scale human colonies in space. At a press conference announcing a contract to his previously low-profile company Blue Origin for development of next-generation engines for US military and spy satellites, Bezos repeated a goal he had given a newspaper reporter as a Florida high school valedictorian: "What we want to have happen is millions of people living and working in space." Yet as the Bezos-owned *Washington Post* also noted of a recent Pew Research report, Americans have more confidence in teleportation (electronic transmission from place to place) than in space colonization. Only a third think space colonies will be a reality within the next 50 years, versus 39 percent for people-beaming. Even the report of the blue-ribbon Review of US Human Spaceflight Plans Committee of 2009, which urged substantial increases in the US space exploration budget, refers to colonies only as small groups of trained astronauts establishing research stations.

One of the pitfalls of becoming a major technological visionary is believing that one can predict and even accomplish the next big thing. Thomas Edison, who held more than a thousand patents on everything from light bulbs to phonographs to motion-picture equipment, plowed his whole fortune from General Electric stock into a failed project for separation of iron from low-grade ore. (He also thought the future of homebuilding was single-pour concrete.) In 1928, Edison's friend and admirer Henry Ford launched a new venture for growing rubber for automobile tires in the Amazon; the venture had lost the equivalent of more than $200 million by the time it ended in 1945.

On the other hand, there are costs in dismissing possibilities. Edison's contemporary, the Scottish physicist William Thomson, who became a peer (first Baron Kelvin), British national hero, and a multimillionaire from innovations that made transatlantic telegraphy possible, is now most often cited for his rejection of an invitation to join the new Aeronautical Society, explaining in a letter that "I have not the smallest molecule of faith in aerial navigation other than ballooning or of expectation of good results from any of the trials we hear of." Yet only ten years later, the Wright Brothers were flying at

Despite talk of colonizing Mars, it is unlikely we'll see space colonies in our lifetime.

Kitty Hawk. Will skepticism about mass space travel look equally foolish in 50 years?

The Risks

Despite cautionary tales of Lord Kelvin and others, most mainstream scientists and engineers are cautious about the prospects for large-scale human colonies in space, especially given current safety concerns. For example, the Review Committee concluded that "although Mars is the ultimate destination for human exploration in the inner solar system, it is not a viable first destination. We do not now have the technology or experience to explore Mars safely and sustainably." One reason, according to the report, is that we have made relatively little progress over 50 years in improving the safety of rocket launches. (The former astronaut and space program advocate Rick Hauck has acknowledged that if he had known there was a 4 percent risk of death for astronauts, he would not have flown.) A recent Government

Accountability Office (GAO) report found serious shortfalls in the program to build a next-generation deep-space rocket and cites the program director's own estimate of a 90 percent chance that it will miss its 2017 launch date. Whether it will be safer or more hazardous than previous designs is still unknown.

Beyond launch safety are the health risks of space flight. Historically the qualms of doctors about the risks of new transportation modes have usually been exaggerated. In his classic book *The Railway Journey*, the historian Wolfgang Schivelbusch quotes 19th-century medical journals on the allegedly deleterious effects of unprecedented speed and vibration on the body. It turned out that many of railroad travel's supposed hazards were imaginary, and the real safety risks were overcome by generations of improvements in construction, signals, and especially air brakes.

But medical specialists have been discovering new risks from space flight faster than they have been finding ways to reduce known ones. The *New York Times* recently reported that while mineral supplements and exercises have overcome the bone loss experienced by early astronauts, research has revealed new and possibly more intractable risks, including lasting deformation of eyeballs, retinal damage, and brain damage from radiation—which can also be an acute hazard in the case of solar storms.

At the 2014 International Astronautical Congress in Toronto, a group of MIT students challenged the Netherlands-based space colonization plan. Among other problems of sustainability, the students claimed, the atmosphere in the artificial environment would begin to be deadly after only about two months. While Bas Lansdorp, Mars One's co-founder, has disputed the accuracy of the students' data, he has acknowledged an additional problem: the lead time needed to resupply life-saving spare parts.

These risks and the "unknown unknowns" don't necessarily doom space colonization. Indeed, in 2013, after the risks to vision were discovered, 200,000 people still applied to live on Mars. The dangers are no greater than that of some earthbound adventure sports like high-altitude mountaineering. Fatality rates are similar to those of Sherpas on Mount Everest. And of course there are likely benefits for the public. For example, just as the original Apollo program led to dozens of high-technology spinoffs, research in space medicine might help prevent and cure some of earth's most serious illnesses, including cancer and eye diseases.

Obstacles and Solutions

The strongest current argument against mass space travel—as opposed to space tourism and conventional astronaut exploration—is the energy and environmental costs of current rockets. It has been calculated that the energy cost of getting a 150-pound person out of the earth's gravitational well works out to $130,000, at today's price of energy per kilowatt-hour, and that is without any of the other costs of hardware and personnel—or the weight of the space capsule and initial equipment and supplies. Space enthusiasts recognize that a serious problem must be overcome: the "tyranny of the rocket equation," in the phrase of the NASA flight engineer Don Pettit. As the Nobel Laureate physicist Edward Purcell once put it to me—I still recall the moment in his office—with the energy needed to put a man into space you could feed him for a lifetime. Carbon emissions are also a major issue for now. According to one environmental site, the Space Shuttle's 113 tons of liquid hydrogen needed 1,360 kwh of energy to produce. Assuming the electricity producing the hydrogen relied on a typical mix of fuel, a single launch was responsible for adding at least 700 tons of CO_2 to the atmosphere.

In the long run there are many theoretically possible ways to overcome costs and environmental objections. The Blue Origin engine may, for example, become far more efficient than existing technology, though so far I have found no energy or environmental specifications on the Blue Origin website. More radically, a Japanese company plans to build a space elevator—a capsule traveling along a cable of still-undeveloped advanced material to an orbiting station or even the Moon—by 2050.

Beyond the many doubts and rejoinders, the real problem of the space colonization movement—as opposed to space exploration and low-orbit commercial space tourism—is in its contradictory premises. Advocates seem to despair about life on the only planet we are sure supports it. (The one exception may be Jeff Bezos, who in his high school interview favored totally evacuating the Earth to make it a nature park.) Most seem to treat space colonization as a form of insurance and some seem to believe, like Stephen Hawking, that climate change or thermonuclear war are likely to do us all in. Yet they also share confidence in the boundless human ingenuity to solve the thorniest problems of space travel and low-gravity living, and in that they may be right. If we are so clever, though, can't we also restore our earthly environment—which is what most people going into space really want to see from above—and feed the world?

Of course there's a possibility that earth is doomed beyond the reach of innovation, yet that technology can be developed that would let millions escape. It's far more likely, however, that in trying to rescue the planet and establish major new space settlements, we would achieve neither.

Thus I side with the masses surveyed in the Pew report against the geniuses. If space colonies are feasible, they'll be unnecessary. And if technological innovation won't save the planet, it also won't let us escape.

EVALUATING THE AUTHOR'S ARGUMENTS:

In this viewpoint, Edward Tenner says that space colonies won't save our planet. Are there reasons to colonize another planet besides escaping Earth? If we could colonize another planet, would it make sense to do so?

Space Travel Is Full of Potential Dangers

"If you've ever been on a long family road trip, you've had a taste of what a trip to Mars might be like."

Jessica Boddy

In the following viewpoint, Jessica Boddy contends that space tourism simply may not be safe. The author lists several of the potential dangers inherent in commercial space travel. Some of these are health challenges, such as damage from cosmic radiation or the risk of disease in a confined space. Others have to do with human nature. Living in a confined space with a small crew for a long time could cause people to become angry and even violent. The stress could also increase the risk of human errors, which can be fatal. Boddy is a news intern with *Science*, a magazine from the American Association for the Advancement of Science.

AS YOU READ, CONSIDER THE FOLLOWING QUESTIONS:
1. Why is cosmic radiation dangerous, according to the article?
2. Why is living without normal gravity a potential problem?
3. How have human errors caused disasters in past space shuttle flights?

From "From shrinking spines to space fungus: The top five dangers of space travel," by Jessica Boddy, American Association for the Advancement of Science, December 2, 2016. (doi:10.1126/science.aal0451) http://www.sciencemag.org/news/2016/12/shrinking-spines-space-fungus-top-five-dangers-space-travel. Reprinted with permission from AAAS.

When President John F. Kennedy declared in 1962 that the United States would go to the moon, not because it is easy, but "because [it is] hard," he had no idea how hard. Nevertheless, the success of the *Apollo 11* moon landing and subsequent manned missions inspired space explorers of all stripes to justify their journeys to other cosmic outposts in the same vein: because it's the ultimate challenge. But with each new study, the passage to Mars and other planets seems fraught with more danger than ever thought possible.

Just lifting off the surface of Earth and landing on another planet is bad enough. But how intense are the dangers of actually traveling in space? Here are five of the most dangerous threats astronauts will face when traveling to Mars and beyond.

Cosmic Radiation

En route to another world, astronauts will be bombarded with cosmic radiation: tiny, high-energy atom fragments that whiz through space and can damage cells and DNA. People on Earth are protected from cosmic rays thanks to Earth's magnetic field, but an unprotected, Mars-bound astronaut would receive 0.3 sieverts of radiation on a one-way trip—that's hardly close to the lethal dose of 8 sieverts or even the radiation sickness–causing dose of 1 sievert, but researchers think that amount (equivalent to 24 computerized tomography scans) is enough to cause irreversible damage to brain cells and other cells that aren't readily replenished.

"The central nervous system is the 800-pound gorilla in all of this," says Charles Limoli, a radiation oncologist at the University of California, Irvine. In a recent rodent study in Scientific Reports, Limoli suggests that cosmic rays would cause long-term brain damage in astronauts on the way to another planet, resulting in dementia, memory deficits, anxiety, depression, and impaired decision-making. "This is not positive news for astronauts deployed on a 2- to 3-year round trip to Mars," he says. But it might be a problem we can fix. Several research groups, including Limoli's, are working on a drug that could protect cells and DNA from being broken apart. Still, others are trying to invent shields that would deflect the rays altogether.

Hurtling through space can take a physical and emotional toll on the traveler.

Going Stir Crazy

If you've ever been on a long family road trip, you've had a taste of what a trip to Mars might be like—except that when your dad plays too much ABBA, you can eventually exit the vehicle. In a years-long deep space voyage without pit stops, a spat could mean life and death for crewmembers. In a NASA-funded report published this year on long space flights, Jack Stuster, a cultural anthropologist at private research corporation Anacapa Sciences in Santa Barbara, California, writes that US astronauts' No. 1 concern on missions to the International Space Station (ISS) was getting along with crew-mates. Their journals, positive overall, reflected that concern: "I think I do need to get out of here," one astronaut wrote. "Living in close quarters with people over a long period of time, definitely even things that normally wouldn't bother you much at all can bother you after a while … that can drive anybody crazy."

And that was when Earth was right out the window. If astronauts start to feel this way when both Earth and their destination are but tiny pinpoints in space, things will feel even grimmer, Stuster says. Though these feelings can be limited by keeping busy, and by the intense psychological screenings that crewmembers undergo, the spectre of violence—and even mutiny—will always be a possibility.

Space Fungus

We've known since the 1960s that some microorganisms can survive the perils of space, including microgravity, extreme temperatures, and radiation. And given that our best efforts to wipe space vessels clean of microorganisms often fails, exposure to these potentially pathogenic organisms is unavoidable. Now, a new study supports that claim. In October, researchers found that the airborne fungus Aspergillus fumigatus, the most common cause of invasive fungal infection in humans, grows just as well on the ISS as it does on Earth. And if fumigatus lives just fine in space, the researchers write, so could many other, more lethal pathogens. The researchers say this calls for a better detection and cleaning policy to avoid sending a ship full of astronauts into the dangers of deep space, only to have them killed by an earthly pathogen.

Microgravity

From YouTube videos of astronauts playing with floating blobs of water or doing effortless backflips, it seems like microgravity would be a blast. But up in space, the reality is much more serious. The absence of gravity causes bones and muscles to deteriorate, leading to a number of physiological problems. Astronauts on the ISS exercise for 2 hours a day to protect their muscles from wasting away, but losing bone density is unavoidable.

Microgravity could also affect the body in other, unpredictable ways. Many astronauts, including Scott Kelly, have returned to Earth with blurred vision. The cause, according to research presented this week at the Radiology Society of North America's annual meeting, is an increased volume of spinal fluid that pushes against the optic nerve and eyeballs, causing farsightedness. In another study, scientists discovered that the spinal muscles of ISS astronauts—essential for support and movement—shrank significantly during their time in space, decreasing by 19%. That could be the reason more than half of all ISS crew members report spinal pain and are four times more likely than Earth-bound citizens to have herniated disks, the researchers write in Spine. One solution? Space yoga—researchers say it might help increase spine mobility and strength. Exactly which poses they'll do is yet to be determined.

FAST FACT

Living without gravity, or with less than normal gravity, can change the human body. Back problems and blurred vision are two of the unpleasant side effects.

Human Error

Making mistakes is something humans are extraordinarily good at, and in space, mistakes tend to hold heavier consequences. Andy Weir, the author of the science-fiction novel *The Martian*, took full advantage of that, crafting his entire plot around how a stranded astronaut must expertly solve dozens of problems or face certain death. Real-life space explorers are not always as lucky. Take the space shuttle *Challenger* and *Columbia* disasters, for example. Both shuttles broke apart because of mechanical problems, killing all seven astronauts on board each time. With *Challenger*, rubber O-rings were the culprit, causing the shuttle to break apart in the sky when they couldn't seal properly in the cold. *Columbia* broke apart during re-entry when insulating foam separated from the shuttle and punctured its left wing. NASA management knew about mechanical issues in both cases, but considered them unimportant because they had never derailed a mission in the past.

On long spaceflights where tensions might be running high or radiation could cause unusual anxiety, depression, or confusion, it'd be no surprise to see human-caused errors like a crash landing, leaky space suits, or even the loss of the water supply. Finding a way to limit the dangers of space and learning from past mistakes will ensure the safest flight to Mars and beyond. And with a little luck, our astronauts could end up as successful as Weir's.

EVALUATING THE AUTHOR'S ARGUMENTS:

In this viewpoint, Jessica Boddy reports on some of the dangers of space travel. These include physical and emotional risks. Do you think the rewards of space travel are worth the risks? Why or why not?

Space Law Needs an Update

Anél Ferreira-Snyman

"It is self-evident that space tourism activities will significantly add to the pollution of both the earth and the outer space environment."

In the following viewpoint, Anél Ferreira-Snyman addresses some legal and environmental challenges of space travel. She states that the Outer Space Treaty does not address modern space travel such as space tourism. Who should be liable for damages from accidents? Who would be responsible for rescuing space tourists in trouble? Pollution is also a problem. Space vehicles emit carbon dioxide, a greenhouse gas that contributes to climate change. They also create debris, or trash left in orbit or in space. Updated international treaties might be necessary before space tourism is a legal and practical possibility. Ferreira-Snyman is a law professor specializing in international space law at the University of South Africa.

AS YOU READ, CONSIDER THE FOLLOWING QUESTIONS:

1. How many people are expected to become space tourists within the next few years, according to sources cited?
2. What is the definition of space tourism, as explained in the article?
3. In what ways might space tourism benefit humanity, according to the article?

Since the Russian Space Agency began to take private persons to the International Space Station (ISS) in 2001 a number of private space tourism companies have been established, especially in recent years. In October 2004 a company, Scaled Composites, won the Ansari X Prize with their space vehicle, SpaceShipOne, by flying past the altitude of 100 kilometres above the earth's surface twice within two weeks while being operated by a civilian pilot and carrying a payload equivalent to two other passengers.

Subsequently Sir Richard Branson's company, Virgin Galactic, announced its plans to take tourists on a 90 minute long journey, costing $200,000 US dollars, into sub-orbital space at three times the speed of sound with its spacecraft, SpaceShipTwo, launching from Spaceport America. SpaceShipTwo performed a successful maiden flight in 2010 and a fleet of these space vehicles is currently under construction.

Space tourism operator, XCOR Aerospace, is developing a rocket-propelled winged vehicle, the Lynx, for passengers who wish to experience an "individualized" half-hour long sub-orbital flight by sitting alongside the pilot, and travelling to an altitude of 100 kilometres. Armadillo Aerospace has plans to develop a sub-orbital two-seater space vehicle called Hyperion. A capsule-styled spacecraft is being developed by Blue Origin, a company owned by Amazon.com co-founder, Jeff Bezos. Excalibur, a space tourism company based on the Isle of Man, plans to place tourists into orbit in the Soviet-made space capsule, Almaz, and to use the Almaz space station as a space hotel.

Other potential space tourism operators include Rocketplane, which plans to offer sub-orbital flights launched out of Dubai, and SpaceX, owned by South African-born Elon Musk, which created a new type of rocket to deliver cargo on behalf of NASA to the International Space Station and which also plans to take private persons into space. The European aerospace company, EADS Astrium, has also announced its plans to provide space tourist flights for groups of four passengers to an altitude of 100 kilometres in a space vehicle named Spaceplane, which will take off and land from a runway.

In order to launch the envisaged commercial space vehicles, the first commercial spaceport, Spaceport America, is currently under

Space debris is just one potential liability that could affect commercial space travel.

construction in New Mexico, while a number of further spaceports are planned in countries such as the United Arab Emirates, Singapore, Sweden, Scotland and the Netherlands Antilles. Significant financial investment is also being made to develop reusable launch vehicle technology for the space tourism industry.

Although space tourism is still in its infancy, it is estimated that the number of space tourists will reach into the hundreds (or, according to Virgin Galactic's predictions, even into the thousands) within the next few years. As space tourist activities increase, accidents will inevitably occur, which will give rise to legal questions relating to the duty of states to rescue space tourists in distress, and the liability for damages. As will be pointed out, the current outer space treaty regime, which focuses on the use of outer space by states, is to a large extent outdated and unable to deal with these questions concerning the private commercial use of space.

Defining Space Tourism

In a broad sense, the term "space tourism" (or "personal space flight") denotes "any commercial activity offering customers direct or indirect experience with space travel". A space tourist has been defined as "someone who tours or travels into, to, or through space or to a celestial body for pleasure and recreation". The possible space tourist activities include long-term stays in orbital facilities for research or entertainment purposes, short-term orbital or sub-orbital flights, and parabolic flights in aircraft where space tourists are exposed to weightless conditions.

In the instance of sub-orbital spaceflight, orbital velocity is not achieved, as the space vehicle re-enters the earth's atmosphere after three to six minutes of microgravity has been achieved. The passengers thus experience a few minutes of weightlessness and the launch vehicle is re-used. The space vehicle is launched either horizontally or vertically and attains an altitude of around 100 kilometers. With orbital spaceflight, orbital velocity must be reached in order to allow the space vehicle to fly along the curvature of the earth without falling back to earth, making it much more energy intensive and thus also technically more difficult and more expensive than sub-orbital spaceflight. Depending on the atmospheric factors, an orbital spacecraft can remain in space for from a few days up to a few years. In the case of intercontinental rocket transport, the idea is to substantially shorten the travel time from one point of the earth to another by transiting through outer space. This form of transport will be specifically useful for the military, as well as for the transportation of persons and goods. There are, however, technical difficulties and safety risks associated with this form of transport. Because of the technological and cost demands of the latter two forms of spaceflight, most personal spaceflights currently on offer will be sub-orbital.

Article I of the Outer Space Treaty requires that the exploration and use of outer space shall be carried out for the benefit and in the interest of all countries. Private human spaceflight may be regarded as a (mostly) recreational activity and, due to the high cost involved, space tourism is currently mainly reserved for the wealthy space travel enthusiast, which makes its benefit for all of mankind unclear. However, space tourism may have certain (long-term) social and economic advantages: Space tourism will most probably eventually lead to more affordable access to space, which could be seen as beneficial for all mankind. In addition, private human spaceflight may have certain social and economic advantages such as the development of new technolo-

gies in the area of human space travel and the boosting of private investment, which could alleviate pressure on the use of public funds for near-earth space exploration. Moreover, if personal spaceflights also serve a scientific purpose by making it possible to carry out scientific experiments under certain space conditions, the benefit for mankind would be obvious.

However, in order to ensure that space tourism activities indeed serve the benefit of all mankind, these activities must be undertaken in a legally regulated as well as an ethical manner. It is self-evident that space tourism activities will significantly add to the pollution of both the earth and the outer space environment. In this regard Masson-Zwaan and Freeland point out that it has been claimed that space tourist vehicles will eventually become the world's primary source of carbon dioxide emissions. An even more immediate problem is that of space debris. No legally binding definition of space debris has, however, been formulated yet. In addition, the space treaties pay very little attention to environmental issues, and the issue of space debris is not specifically addressed in the Outer Space Treaty (nor in any of the other space treaties), as these issues were not high on the agenda of the space-faring nations at the time of the conclusion of the treaties. At present, the mitigation of space debris is a matter of the voluntary compliance of states with the space debris mitigation guidelines and national legal rules in this regard. In view of the increasing commercial use of outer space, including the planned space tourism ventures, it is imperative that this problem is addressed as a matter of urgency, as it could significantly hamper the future exploration and use of space.

The Way Forward?

It should be clear from the above exposition that the current space treaties are to a large extent outdated and that they cannot adequately deal with the unique legal challenges presented by the rapidly developing space tourism industry. This is furthermore exacerbated by the fact that the outer space legal framework is very fragmented—consisting of treaties, UN principles and guidelines, regional regulations and intergovernmental agreements, as well as national guidelines and legislation.

In order to ensure that space tourism is indeed to the benefit of all mankind, it is imperative that clear international legal rules relating to space tourism are formulated, where standards are set for the authorisation and supervision of these activities, and the interests of states, passengers and private actors are balanced as far as possible.

EVALUATING THE AUTHOR'S ARGUMENTS:

In this viewpoint, Anél Ferreira-Snyman claims that new treaties are needed to regulate space travel. Should space travel be left to individual countries and companies, or regulated internationally? Why?

The Risks and Rewards of Sending People into Space

Joshua Colwell and Daniel Britt

"The manned exploration of space is an expression of one of our finest aspects— curiosity."

In the following viewpoint, Joshua Colwell and Daniel Britt argue about the future of space exploration. Colwell claims that humans should go into space to explore. In his view, the inspiration provided by sending people into space has its own value. He also fears that funding would be cut if space exploration was conducted purely for scientific purposes. Britt, on the other hand, notes that it is safer and cheaper to send robots into space. Both authors agree that the space program should include both human and robotic exploration. Colwell, PhD, and Britt, PhD, are both professors at the University of Central Florida and work on projects with NASA.

AS YOU READ, CONSIDER THE FOLLOWING QUESTIONS:
1. What are the advantages of sending humans into space?
2. What are some disadvantages of sending humans into space?
3. How does sending robots into space help prepare for future flights with humans?

"Robots vs Astronauts," by Joshua Colwell and Daniel Britt, University of Central Florida. Reprinted by permission.

W"e choose to go to the moon in this decade and do the other things, not because they are easy, but because they are hard." With these words, President John F. Kennedy roused America's support of space exploration in 1962. He also acknowledged the geopolitical competition with the Soviet Union that provided the impetus to make mankind's greatest technological achievement a possibility. Absent that Cold War motivation, our manned space program has languished in low Earth orbit for the last 40 years. That drought drives home the point that we must return to the spirit of human exploration of the final frontier exemplified by the Apollo program. The need to see what is over the next horizon—and not to simply see it, but to actually touch it—is a fundamental aspect of human nature. Those horizons beckon on countless asteroids, the moon and Mars.

Humans Are Essential for Space Exploration

The manned exploration of space is an expression of one of our finest aspects—curiosity. To truly satisfy that curiosity we need to be participants. My colleague correctly points out that the robotic space program is a far more cost-effective means of advancing our scientific knowledge of the universe, and I could not agree more. While valuable advances have been made because of the manned program, it cannot and should not be justified on the grounds of scientific advancement. It is instead about something equally important as science—the inspiration of our species to pursue lofty goals.

Space scientists frequently make the mistake of assuming that the space exploration budget is a zero-sum game, lamenting the money spent on the manned program that could be used to fund ambitious and scientifically valuable robotic missions. It is naïve to expect that politicians would spend those same billions on purely scientific exploration. If the manned program was canceled today, its budget would disappear, never to be spent on space exploration of any kind. In contrast, the US manned space program enables NASA to maintain a scientific program of space exploration that is by far the largest in the world. We need to move past the debate of manned versus unmanned programs and recognize that they serve different yet complementary roles, and that each endeavor ultimately strengthens the other.

A NASA astronaut poses with Robonaut 2, the dexterous humanoid astronaut helper, in the International Space Station.

Robots Are Key to Future Space Exploration

On the plus side, humans in space provide operational flexibility, inspiration and native intelligence. On the minus side, that flexibility comes at a steep price. Humans are heavy, fragile, dirty, vulnerable, picky about their environment, and have a low tolerance for the space environment (i.e., high energy radiation, extreme heat and cold, etc.).

The fragility of humans, our aversion for risking human life, and the all-too-human need for consumables (food, water and oxygen) require vast amounts of money to pay for the extra engineering and multiple redundant systems we demand to reduce risk to astronauts, as well as for the vastly larger support crews needed to baby-sit every aspect of daily life during a manned space mission.

For crewed spacecraft, Venus and Mercury are impossibly hot, and the asteroid belt and Jupiter are impossibly cold. The longer travel times to these worlds would be a death sentence from radiation exposure, not to mention bone loss and muscle atrophy. Once at an exploration target, humans can be a mixed blessing. Imagine trying to search for life on Mars with human explorers who are shedding pollutants and terrestrial contamination with literally every step and breath.

Fundamentally there is no real choice between robotic and human exploration of space, however. Both are synergistic and mutually dependent. Robotic exploration is necessary to enable human exploration by setting the context, providing critical information, and reducing the risk to humans. Imagine how the Apollo program would have functioned without its robotic precursors—Lunar Orbiter to map the moon's surface, Ranger to get close-up views of areas that helped perfect NASA's navigation skills (remember that NASA missed the moon with two of the first three Rangers to get that far), and Surveyor to explore the surface, determine its composition and practice soft landings. Without these robotic precursors it would've been impossible to know where to go on the moon, to design the landing hardware, or to have any real idea of what to do once we got there—other than plant the flag.

Is there a choice between human and robotic exploration? Not really. Considering the current limited range of human exploration, robotic exploration is essential to enable manned missions. For the rest of the solar system, robotic exploration is the only realistic game in town.

Chapter 3

Are We Going to the Moon or to Mars?

Will your vacation photos look like this in the future?

We Can Return to the Moon— to Live

Matt Williams

> *"The proposed lunar base would exist at one of the poles and would be modeled on the US Antarctic Station at the South Pole."*

In the following viewpoint, Matt Williams assesses the possibility of establishing a human settlement on the moon. A moon base would allow for important long-term research on the moon. It would also make it easier to explore more distant space. The author notes that funding for such a colony is one obstacle, but that new technologies are lowering costs. Williams suggests that a moon base would require an international partnership. It also would involve both government agencies and private companies. Williams is a writer for Universe Today, a space and astronomy news website.

AS YOU READ, CONSIDER THE FOLLOWING QUESTIONS:

1. When did the first astronauts reach the moon?
2. What are the benefits to establishing a base on the moon, according to the article?
3. How soon might people return to the moon, according to predictions mentioned in the article?

"Moonbase by 2022 for $10 Billion, Says NASA," by Matt Williams, Universe Today, April 12, 2016. Reprinted by permission.

Establishing a long-term research base on the moon would open the door to missions to other parts of space as well.

Returning to the Moon has been the fevered dream of many scientists and astronauts. Ever since the Apollo Program culminated with the first astronauts setting foot on the Moon on July 20th, 1969, we have been looking for ways to go back to the Moon … and to stay there. In that time, multiple proposals have been drafted and considered. But in every case, these plans failed, despite the brave words and bold pledges made.

However, in a workshop that took place in August of 2014, representatives from NASA met with Harvard geneticist George Church, Peter Diamandis from the X Prize Foundation and other parties invested in space exploration to discuss low-cost options for returning to the Moon. The papers, which were recently made available in a special issue of *New Space*, describe how a settlement could be built on the Moon by 2022, and for the comparatively low cost of $10 billion.

Put simply, there are many benefits to establishing a base on the Moon. In addition to providing refueling stations that would shave billions off of future space missions—especially to Mars, which are planned for the 2030s—they would provide unique opportunities for scientific research and the testing of new technologies. But plans to build one have consistently been hampered by two key assumptions.

The Assumptions

The first is that funding is the largest hurdle to overcome, which is understandable given the past 50 years of space mission costs. To put it in perspective, the Apollo Program would cost taxpayers approximately $150 billion in today's dollars. Meanwhile, NASA's annual budget for 2015 was approximately $18 billion, while its 2016 is projected to reach $19.3 billion. In the days when space exploration is not a matter of national security, money is sure to be more scarce.

The second assumption is that a presidential mandate to "return to the Moon to stay" is all that is needed overcome this problem and make the necessary budgets available. But despite repeated attempts, no mandate for renewed lunar or space exploration has resolved the issue. In short, space exploration is hampered by conventional think-ing that assumes massive budgets are needed and that administra-tions simply need to make them available.

In truth, a number of advances that have been made in recent years are allowing for missions that would cost significantly less. This, and how a lunar base could be a benefit to space exploration and humanity, were the topics of discussion at the 2014 workshop. As NASA astrobiologist Chris McKay—who edited the *New Space* jour-nal series—told Universe Today via email, one of the key benefits of a cost-effective base on the Moon is that it will bring other missions into the realm of affordability.

"I am interested in a long term research base on Mars—not just a short term human landing," he said. "Establishing a research base on the Moon shows that we know how to do that and can do it in a sustainable way. We have to get away from the current situation where costs are so high that a base on the Moon, a human mission to Mars, and a human mission to an asteroid are all mutually exclusive. If we can drive the costs down by 10x or more then we can do them all."

Central to this are several key changes that have taken place over the past decade. These include the development of the space launch business, which has led to an overall reduction in the cost of individual launches. The emergence of the NewSpace industry—i.e. a general term for various private commercial aerospace ventures—is another, which has been taking recent advances in technology and finding applications for them in space.

According to McKay, these and other technological developments will help resolve the budget issue. "Beyond the launch costs, they key to driving down the costs for a base on the Moon is to make use of technologies for sustainability being developed on Earth. My favorite examples are 3D printing, electric-cars, autonomous robots, and recycling toilets (like the blue diversion toilet)."

Alexandra Hall, the former Senior Director of the X Prize Foundation and one of the series' main authors, also expressed the importance of emerging technologies in making this lunar base functional. As she told Universe Today via email, these will have significant benefits here on Earth, especially in the coming decades where rises in population will coincide with diminishing resources.

"The advances in life support and closed loop living necessary for sustaining life for long periods on the Moon will undoubtedly provide positive spin offs that benefit both the environment and our ability to live with changing climate and diminishing resources," she said. "If we can figure out how to build structures with what's already on the Moon, we can use that technology to help us create infrastructure and shelter solutions out of in-situ materials on Earth. If we can use rock that's right there, perhaps we can avoid shipping asphalt and bricks across the world!"

International Partnerships

Another important aspect of making a lunar base cost-effective was the potential for international partnerships, as well as those between the private and public sectors. As Hall explained it:

While there will be commercial markets for the eventual fruits of our lunar exploration endeavors, the initial markets are likely to be dominated by governments. The private sector is best able to respond in ways that provide cost effective and competitive solutions when governments specify and commit to long term exploration goals. I believe that a Google Lunar XPRIZE win will flush out other private and commercial partners for pursuing a permanent settlement on the Moon, that could eclipse the need for significant government participation. Once a small company demonstrates that it is actually possible to get to the Moon and be productive, that allows others to start to plan new business and endeavors.

As for where this base will go and what it will do, that is described in the preface article, "Toward a Low-Cost Lunar Settlement." In essence, the proposed lunar base would exist at one of the poles and would be modeled on the US Antarctic Station at the South Pole. It would be operated by NASA or an international consortium and house a crew of about 10 people, a mix of staff and field scientists that would be rotated three times a year.

Activities on the base, which would be assisted by autonomous and remotely-operated robotic devices, would center on supporting field research, mainly by graduate students doing thesis work. Another key activity for the residents would be testing technologies and program precedents which could be put to use on Mars, where NASA hopes to be sending astronauts in the coming decades.

Several times over in the series, it is stressed that this can be done for the relatively low cost of $10 billion. This overall assessments is outlined in the paper titled "A Summary of the Economic Assessment and Systems Analysis of an Evolvable Lunar Architecture That Leverages Commercial Space Capabilities and Public–Private Partner". As it concludes:

Based on the experience of recent NASA program innovations, such as the COTS program, a human return to the Moon may not be as expensive as previously thought. The United States could lead a return of humans to the surface of the

Moon within a period of 5–7 years from authority to proceed at an estimated total cost of about $10 billion (–30%) for two independent and competing commercial service providers, or about $5 billion for each provider, using partnership methods."

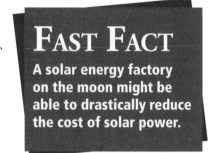

FAST FACT

A solar energy factory on the moon might be able to drastically reduce the cost of solar power.

Other issues discussed in the series are the location of the base and the nature of its life-support systems. In the article titled "Site Selection for Lunar Industrialization, Economic Development, and Settlement", the case is made for a base located in either the northern or southern polar region. Written by Dennis Whigo, founder and CEO of Skycorp, the article identifies two potential sites for a lunar base, using input parameters developed in consultation with venture capitalists.

These include the issues of power availability, low-cost communications over wide areas, availability of possible water (or hydrogen-based molecules) and other resources, and surface mobility. According to these assessments, the northern polar region is a good location because of its ample access to solar power. The southern pole is also identified as a potential site (particularly in the Shackleton Crater) due to the presence of water ice.

Economic Benefits

Last, but certainly not least, the series explores the issue of economic opportunities that could have far-ranging benefits for people here on Earth. Foremost among these is the potential for creating space solar power (SSP), a concept which has been explored as a possible solution to humanity's reliance on fossil fuels and the limits of Earth-based solar power.

Whereas Earth-based solar collectors are limited by meteorological phenomena (i.e. weather) and Earth's diurnal cycle (night and day), solar collectors placed in orbit would be able to collect energy from the Sun around the clock. However, the issues of launch and wireless energy transmission costs make this option financially unattractive.

But as is laid out in "Lunar-Based Self-Replicating Solar Factory", establishing a factory on the Moon could reduce costs by a factor of four. This factory could build solar power satellites out of lunar material, using a self-replicating system (SRS) able to construct replicas of itself, then deploy them into geostationary Earth orbit via a linear electromagnetic accelerator (aka. Mass Driver).

An overriding theme in the series is how a lunar base would present opportunities for cooperation, both between the private and public sectors and different nations. The ISS is repeatedly used an example, which has benefited greatly in the past decade from programs like NASA's Commercial Orbital Transportation Services (COTS)—which has been very successful at acquiring cost-effective transportation service to the station.

It is therefore understandable why NASA and those companies that have benefited from COTS want to extend this model to the Moon—in what is often referred to as Lunar Commercial Orbital Transfer Services (LCOTS) program. Aside from establishing a human presence on the Moon, this endeavor is being undertaken with the knowledge that it will also push the development of technologies and capabilities that could lead to an affordable to Mars in the coming years.

It sure is an exciting idea: returning to the Moon and laying the groundwork for a permanent human settlement there. It is also exciting when considered in the larger context of space exploration, how a base on the Moon will help us to reach further into space. To Mars, to the Asteroid Belt, perhaps to the outer Solar System and beyond.

And with each step, the opportunities for resource utilization and scientific research will expand accordingly. It may sounds like the stuff of dreams; but then again, so did the idea of putting a man on the Moon before the end of the 1960s. If there's one thing that particular experience taught us, it's that setting foot on another world leaves lasting footprints!

EVALUATING THE AUTHOR'S ARGUMENTS:

In this viewpoint, Matt Williams discusses the benefits of building a base on the moon. The article is largely optimistic about this happening. Given the challenges, does it seem likely that people will return to the moon within a few years?

2

We Can Colonize Mars (Eventually)

Matt Williams

"The challenges to creating a permanent settlement on Mars are numerous, but not necessarily insurmountable."

In the following viewpoint, Matt Williams addresses the challenges of colonizing Mars. The planet Mars is similar to Earth in several ways, including the length of its days and its seasons. Of the two planets closest to Earth, Mars is by far the most habitable, or suitable for life. However, Mars is different from Earth in ways that would cause problems. Mars has less gravity and the atmosphere is not breathable by humans. William suggests that people may be able to colonize Mars, but it won't be easy. Matt Williams writes for for Universe Today and is also the author of the previous viewpoint.

AS YOU READ, CONSIDER THE FOLLOWING QUESTIONS:
1. What is the average surface temperature on Mars?
2. What are the benefits to a colony on Mars, according to the article?
3. Approximately how long would it take to get to Mars at the ideal time, according to the article?

"Will We Ever Colonize Mars?" by Matt Williams, Phys.org, June 1, 2015.

Mars. It's a pretty unforgiving place. On this dry, dessicated world, the average surface temperature is -55 °C (-67 °F). And at the poles, temperatures can reach as low as -153 °C (243 °F). Much of that has to do with its thin atmosphere, which is too thin to retain heat (not to mention breathe). So why then is the idea of colonizing Mars so intriguing to us?

Well, there are a number of reasons, which include the similarities between our two planets, the availability of water, the prospects for generating food, oxygen, and building materials on-site. And there's even the long-term benefits of using Mars as a source of raw materials and terraforming it into a liveable environment. Let's go over them one by one …

Benefits

As already mentioned, there are many interesting similarities between Earth and Mars that make it a viable option for colonization. For starters, Mars and Earth have very similar lengths of days. A Martian day is 24 hours and 39 minutes, which means that plants and animals—not to mention human colonists—would find that familiar.

Mars also has an axial tilt that is very similar to Earth's, which means it has the same basic seasonal patterns as our planet (albeit for longer periods of time). Basically, when one hemisphere is pointed towards the Sun, it experiences summer while the other experiences winter—complete with warmer temperatures and longer days.

This too would work well when it comes to growing seasons and would provide colonists with a comforting sense of familiarity and a way of measuring out the year. Much like farmers here on Earth, native Martians would experience a "growing season", a "harvest", and would be able to hold annual festivities to mark the changing of the seasons.

Also, much like Earth, Mars exists within our Sun's habitable zone (aka. "goldilocks zone"), though it is slightly towards its outer edge. Venus is similarly located within this zone, but its location on the inner edge (combined with its thick atmosphere) has led to it becoming the hottest planet in the Solar System. That, combined with its sulfuric acid rains makes Mars a much more attractive option.

Experts have envisioned human settlements on Mars.

Additionally, Mars is closer to Earth than the other Solar planets—except for Venus, but we already covered why it's not a very good option! This would make the process of colonizing it easier. In fact, every few years when the Earth and Mars are at opposition—i.e. when they are closest to each other—the distance varies, making certain "launch windows" ideal for sending colonists.

For example, on April 8th, 2014, Earth and Mars were 92.4 million km (57.4 million miles) apart at opposition. On May 22nd, 2016, they will be 75.3 million km (46.8 million miles) apart, and by July 27th of 2018, a meager 57.6 million km (35.8 million miles) will separate our two worlds. During these windows, getting to Mars would be a matter of months rather than years.

Also, Mars has vast reserves of water in the form of ice. Most of this water ice is located in the polar regions, but surveys of Martian meteorites have suggested that much of it may also be locked away beneath the surface. This water could be extracted and purified for human consumption easily enough.

In his book, *The Case for Mars*, Robert Zubrin also explains how future human colonists might be able to live off the land when traveling to Mars, and eventually colonize it. Instead of bringing all their supplies from Earth—like the inhabitants of the International Space

Station—future colonists would be able to make their own air, water, and even fuel by splitting Martian water into oxygen and hydrogen.

Preliminary experiments have shown that Mars soil could be baked into bricks to create protective structures, which would cut down on the amount of materials needed to be shipped to the surface. Earth plants could eventually be grown in Martian soil too, assuming they get enough sunlight and carbon dioxide. Over time, planting on the native soil could also help to create a breathable atmosphere.

Challenges

Despite the aforementioned benefits, there are also some rather monumental challenges to colonizing the Red Planet. For starters, there is the matter of the average surface temperature, which is anything but hospitable. While temperatures around the equator at midday can reach a balmy 20 °C, at the Curiosity site—the Gale Crater, which is close to the equator—typical nighttime temperatures are as low as -70 °C.

The gravity on Mars is also only about 40% of what we experience on Earth's, which would make adjusting to it quite difficult. According to a NASA report, the effects of zero-gravity on the human body are quite profound, with a loss of up to 5% muscle mass a week and 1% of bone density a month.

Naturally, these losses would be lower on the surface of Mars, where there is at least some gravity. But permanent settlers would still have to contend with the problems of muscle degeneration and osteoporosis in the long run.

And then there's the atmosphere, which is unbreathable. About 95% of the planet's atmosphere is carbon dioxide, which means that in addition to producing breathable air for their habitats, settlers would also not be able to go outside without a pressure suit and bottled oxygen.

Mars also has no global magnetic field comparable to Earth's geomagnetic field. Combined with a thin atmosphere, this means that a significant amount of ionizing radiation is able to reach the Martian surface.

Thanks to measurements taken by the Mars Odyssey spacecraft's

Mars Radiation Environment Experiment (MARIE), scientists learned that radiation levels in orbit above Mars are 2.5 times higher than at the International Space Station. Levels on the surface would be lower, but would still be higher than human beings are accustomed to.

In fact, a recent paper submitted by a group of MIT researchers—which analyzed the Mars One plan to colonize the planet beginning in 2020—concluded that the first astronaut would suffocate after 68 days, while the others would die from a combination of starvation, dehydration, or incineration in an oxygen-rich atmosphere.

In short, the challenges to creating a permanent settlement on Mars are numerous, but not necessarily insurmountable.

Terraforming

Over time, many or all of the difficulties in living on Mars could be overcome through the application of geoengineering (aka. terraforming). Using organisms like cyanobacteria and phytoplankton, colonists could gradually convert much of the CO_2 in the atmosphere into breathable oxygen.

In addition, it is estimated that there is a significant amount of carbon dioxide (CO_2) in the form of dry ice at the Martian south pole, not to mention absorbed by in the planet's regolith (soil). If the temperature of the planet were raised, this ice would sublimate into gas and increase atmospheric pressure. Although it would still not be breathable by humans, it would be sufficient enough to eliminate the need for pressure suits.

A possible way of doing this is by deliberately triggering a greenhouse effect on the planet. This could be done by importing ammonia ice from the atmospheres of other planets in our Solar System. Because ammonia (NH_3) is mostly nitrogen by weight, it could also supply the buffer gas needed for a breathable atmosphere—much as it does here on Earth.

Similarly, it would be possible to trigger a greenhouse effect by importing hydrocarbons like methane—which is common in Titan's atmosphere and on its surface. This methane could be vented into the atmosphere where it would act to compound the greenhouse effect.

Zubrin and Chris McKay, an astrobiologist with NASA's Ames

Research center, have also suggested creating facilities on the surface that could pump greenhouse gases into the atmosphere, thus triggering global warming (much as they do here on Earth).

Other possibilities exist as well, ranging from orbital mirrors that would heat the surface to deliberately impacting the surface with comets. But regardless of the method, possibilities exist for transforming Mars' environment that could make it more suitable for humans in the long run—many of which we are currently doing right here on Earth (with less positive results).

Another proposed solution is building habitats underground. By building a series of tunnels that connect between subterranean habitats, settlers could forgo the need for oxygen tanks and pressure suits when they are away from home.

Additionally, it would provide protection against radiation exposure. Based on data obtained by the Mars Reconnaissance Orbiter, it is also speculated that habitable environments exist underground, making it an even more attractive option.

Proposed Missions

NASA's proposed manned mission to Mars—which is slated to take place during the 2030s using the Orion Multi-Purpose Crew Vehicle (MPCV) and the Space Launch System (SLS)—is not the only proposal to send humans to the Red Planet. In addition to other federal space agencies, there are also plans by private corporations and non-profits, some of which are far more ambitious than mere exploration.

The European Space Agency (ESA) has long-term plans to send humans, though they have yet to build a manned spacecraft. Roscosmos, the Russian Federal Space Agency, is also planning a manned Mars mission, with simulations (called Mars-500) having been completed in Russia back in 2011. The ESA is currently participating in these simulations as well.

In 2012, a group of Dutch entrepreneurs revealed plans for a crowdfunded campaign to establish a human Mars base, beginning in 2023. Known as MarsOne, the plan calls for a series of one-way missions to establish a permanent and expanding colony on Mars, which would be financed with the help of media participation.

Other details of the MarsOne plan include sending a telecom orbiter by 2018, a rover in 2020, and the base components and its settlers by 2023. The base would be powered by 3,000 square meters of solar panels and the SpaceX Falcon 9 Heavy rocket would be used to launch the hardware. The first crew of 4 astronauts would land on Mars in 2025; then, every two years, a new crew of 4 astronauts would arrive.

On December 2nd, 2014, NASA's Advanced Human Exploration Systems and Operations Mission Director Jason Crusan and Deputy Associate Administrator for Programs James Reuthner announced tentative support for the Boeing "Affordable Mars Mission Design". Currently planned for the 2030s, the mission profile includes plans for radiation shielding, centrifugal artificial gravity, in-transit consumable resupply, and a return-lander.

SpaceX and Tesla CEO Elon Musk has also announced plans to establish a colony on Mars with a population of 80,000 people. Intrinsic to this plan is the development of the Mars Colonial Transporter (MCT), a spaceflight system that would rely of reusable rocket engines, launch vehicles and space capsules to transport humans to Mars and return to Earth.

As of 2014, SpaceX has begun development of the large Raptor rocket engine for the Mars Colonial Transporter, but the MCT is not expected to be operational until the mid-2020s. In January 2015, Musk said that he hoped to release details of the "completely new architecture" for the Mars transport system in late 2015.

There may come a day when, after generations of terraforming and numerous waves of colonists, that Mars will begin to have a viable economy as well. This could take the form of mineral deposits being discovered and then sent back to Earth for sale. Launching precious metals, like platinum, off the surface of Mars would be relatively inexpensive thanks to its lower gravity.

But according to Musk, the most likely scenario (at least for the foreseeable future) would involve an economy based on real estate. With human populations exploding all over Earth, a new destination that offers plenty of room to expand is going to look like a good investment. And once transportation issues are worked out, savvy investors are likely to start buying up land.

Plus, there is likely to be a market for scientific research on Mars for centuries to come. Who knows what we might find once planetary surveys really start to open up!

In short, one day, there could be real Martians—and they would be us!

EVALUATING THE AUTHOR'S ARGUMENTS:

In this viewpoint, Matt Williams notes several challenges to building a colony on Mars. Given this information, does it seem likely that people will colonize Mars? If so, is it likely to happen in the time frame suggested by some plans?

NASA Isn't Going to Mars Anytime Soon

Eric Berger

"The nation's approach will have to be fundamentally changed if we are to succeed."

In the following viewpoint, Eric Berger examines the cost of sending astronauts to Mars. This article, published about six months after the previous viewpoint, reviews a NASA report. The report did not address the cost of a human mission to Mars, but Berger quotes other opinions on the expense. To reach Mars, NASA might have to dedicate all its resources to a Mars mission. By doing that, the organization would risk losing everything if political priorities change. In the end, Berger says, a mission to Mars will require strong leadership determined to reach Mars, and we may not have that. Eric Berger is a science writer with the *Houston Chronicle* newspaper.

AS YOU READ, CONSIDER THE FOLLOWING QUESTIONS:

1. How much is NASA's budget for human space exploration?
2. According to the industry sources cited, how much will it cost to land astronauts on Mars?
3. When does Mark Albrecht believe astronauts could reach Mars, according to the article?

"NASA Finally Talks Mars Budget, and it's Not Enough," by Eric Berger, Hearst Newspapers, LLC., January 8, 2016. Reprinted by permission.

O n Thursday NASA released a glossy 35-page report on its "Journey to Mars," reaffirming its intent to put human boots in the planet's red, dusty soil by the 2030s.

But the plan did not address the specific cost of a human mission to the Red Planet, which has been standard practice for the space agency in the five years it has been talking about it.

To get some idea of how NASA intends to pay for its Martian dream, one would have had to be in attendance at a Space Transportation Association luncheon on Capitol Hill earlier in the week where Robert Lightfoot, NASA's associate administrator, essentially declared it could be done without raising the agency's current budget.

That may have been the analysis Congress, which has more or less held NASA's human exploration budget steady at $8 billion annually and is disinclined to raise it, wanted to hear. But it also probably means NASA isn't going to Mars any time soon.

The National Research Council has studied this budget scenario in depth and concluded in its 2014 Pathways to Exploration report that "With current flat or even inflation-adjusted budget projections for human spaceflight, there are no viable pathways to Mars."

At the Capitol Hill luncheon, Lightfoot said a Mars program would have to be accomplished with a budget that is one-tenth of the budget that sent Apollo astronauts to the moon.

"From a NASA perspective it'll be done for about one-tenth of the budget that we were doing back then," Lightfoot said, according to Space News.

Congress Frustrated

A NASA spokeswoman said after Lightfoot's speech that he was comparing the Apollo budget and the agency's current budget based on percentages of the overall federal budget. NASA received 4 percent of the total federal budget during the height of the Apollo Program, and today NASA has 0.4 percent.

"We intend to carry out our current ambitious exploration plans within current budget levels, with modest increases aligned to economic growth," NASA's Lauren Worley said.

The release of the "Journey to Mars" report that contained no specific budget for a Mars mission frustrated some members of Congress.

How much will a human mission to Mars cost? The lack of an answer to that question has stalled progress.

"Regrettably, this proposal contains no budget," Lamar Smith, a San Antonio Republican who chairs the House Science Committee, said Friday. "It contains no schedule, no deadlines. It's just some real pretty photographs and some nice words. That is … not going to get us to Mars."

Another Republican, Dana Rohrabacher, of California, was more blunt: "We don't even have a budget? This is insane."

In declaring that with the current budget there are no "viable pathways to Mars," the National Research Council cited several reasons. Among them are the high costs of developing Mars hardware, low flight rates—if NASA doesn't fly often stakeholders wonder what it is doing, and it's difficult to keep employees engaged—and maintaining a program across multiple presidential administrations.

With its current human exploration budget, plus inflation, the influential Pathways report found that the agency would only accumulate about $100 billion between now and 2040 for Mars-related work.

Without a clearly defined plan or the types of rockets, spacecraft and landers needed to pull it off, it is impossible to estimate how much it would cost to land astronauts on Mars. But industry sources offer rough estimates that, using NASA's current practices, the cost is likely between $200 billion and $400 billion.

A Daunting Task

Last year Mitch Daniels, the former Indiana Governor and current Purdue University president who co-led the Pathways report, said what struck him most during the process of researching and writing was how incredibly daunting it would be to reach Mars, both from an engineering and political standpoint.

"The nation's approach will have to be fundamentally changed if we are to succeed," Daniels said. "I don't think most amateurs like me understand how steep those challenges are."

Mark Albrecht, an aerospace executive and principal space adviser to President George H.W. Bush, does. He was part of Bush's team that, in 1990, tried to set NASA on a course to Mars.

That effort failed when NASA submitted a report that called for a tripling of its budget to eventually land humans on Mars.

Albrecht said NASA, now with a total annual budget of more than $18 billion, has enough funds to pull off a Mars mission.

"NASA has enough money, more than enough money," he said. "The problem is it is spent on a jillion different things."

When it comes to setting the budget, the agency spends billions on space science, Earth science, airplane technology and education.

All may be worthy investments, but if NASA set Mars as its core goal and turned all of its field centers toward that aim, it could reach the red planet by the 2030s, Albrecht said.

But NASA's leaders, Albrecht said, are worried that if they go all in for a human mission to Mars the next president could come in, cancel that program, and there would be nothing left of the agency.

"The problem with that attitude is, essentially, NASA's leaders are saying the existence and sustainability of the organization is their number one priority," he said.

Leadership Needed

Breaking that mold would require strong, committed presidential leadership. NASA has really only had that kind of sustained direction from a president once, under John F. Kennedy, who propelled the agency to the moon.

A couple of years ago the JFK Library released some tapes from 1962 in which Kennedy confronted NASA's administrator at the time, James Webb. This was a month after Kennedy's "We Choose to go to the Moon" speech.

During the exchange Kennedy makes clear to Webb that the primary goal is to safely send men to the moon and back.

Webb replies that there's a lot of science that goes along with that, and that the scientific community isn't going to be happy if this is simply an engineering exercise. The scientists want to learn a lot more about space and other things.

"If I go out and say this is the number one priority and everything else must give way to it, I'm going to lose an important element of support," Webb says.

"By whom? Who? Who?" Kennedy asks.

Particularly the "brainy people," Webb replies.

Kennedy is having none of it. "We ought to be clear," Kennedy says. "Otherwise we shouldn't be spending this money because I'm not that interested in space."

EVALUATING THE AUTHOR'S ARGUMENTS:

In this viewpoint, Eric Berger expresses skepticism that NASA will successfully land astronauts on Mars anytime soon. How does this attitude compare to the previous viewpoint? With this additional information, has your opinion changed?

It's a Long, Hard Road to Mars

Mia Brown

> *"It is not whether or not the technology can be built, but a matter of will it be built."*

In the following viewpoint, Mia Brown reports on a meeting of the international space community. In particular, she addresses plans by Elon Musk of SpaceX to build a city on Mars. She notes that with private space companies dependent on NASA for funding, they must also follow NASA regulations. As a government agency, NASA is less likely to take risks, which may limit private companies associated with NASA. Other challenges include the very high expense, and the new technology needed. Mia Brown is a Research Associate at the Space Studies Board of the National Academies of Sciences, Engineering, and Medicine, nonprofit institutions.

AS YOU READ, CONSIDER THE FOLLOWING QUESTIONS:
1. When does Elon Musk, CEO of SpaceX, hope to build a city on Mars?
2. What is the relationship between SpaceX and NASA?
3. How much will it cost to send a person to Mars, if the ultimate goal can be met?

"The view from tomorrow: Challenges to regulating commercial space travel," by Mia Brown, The Brookings Institution, September 30, 2016. Reprinted by permission.

SpaceX CEO Elon Musk unveiled the Manned Dragon V2 Space Taxi in 2014. Musk is just one entrepreneur with plans to develop sustainable living on Mars.

Members of the international space community recently gathered in Guadalajara, Mexico for the 2016 International Astronautical Congress (IAC) to discuss current and emerging issues in the space sector. This year in particular, major launch providers took the opportunity to provide critical updates on their plans to develop the next wave of innovative launch vehicles.

Recent trends have pointed space launch in the direction of reusable launch vehicles, reaching the outer limits of what was once only possible in science fiction stories. We've seen increases in launch competition with "NewSpace" companies such as Blue Origin, SpaceX, and Virgin Galactic, while United Launch Alliance and Arianespace are continuing their efforts to create the next competitive vehicle.

In a much anticipated keynote presentation, Elon Musk, CEO of SpaceX, laid out his plans to build a sustainable city on Mars within the next forty to one hundred years. His argument for Mars follows many long and arduous debates within the international space community on how to break new grounds in space exploration in a post-Shuttle era. Priorities and opportunities vary widely in the commercial space sector, but competition is still very much a reality for the few commercial companies trying to enter a limited market in the future. In remarks given at IAC, George Whitesides, CEO of Virgin Galactic, expressed the importance of the planetary perspective and echoed the sentiments of Buckminster Fuller, where Earth is a moving spaceship that needs to be protected. When asked if there was any interest in Mars, Whitesides responded that while nothing is out of the question, focus now should be on increasing access to space, while decreasing the costs that are more practical.

When it comes down to the determining factor, it is not whether or not the technology can be built, but a matter of will it be built. Technological prowess does not override the many regulatory and budgetary hurdles that are very much a reality for such large-scale projects. SpaceX depends heavily on funding from NASA's Commercial Crew Program. Current Space Act Agreements between the company and NASA provide SpaceX with the opportunity to deliver crew and cargo to the International Space Station. Even if the company begins crew missions to the ISS as early as 2018, this would not translate to providing transport to Mars.

Musk has yet to address the human aspect of human spaceflight, when he left out how his company plans to address safety issues for living on Mars. He briefly spoke about the risks in human spaceflight to Mars during the Q and A session and hesitated to go into further detail regarding how, once passengers arrive on the red planet, they plan to survive there. The risks automatically rise when there are humans involved. Whitesides exclaimed that risk is the primary differences between NewSpace and government. NewSpace companies are able to take a significantly greater amount of risk, while government agencies like NASA cannot. Especially with the large amount of funding NASA supports SpaceX with, their programs will need to adhere to the agency's standards.

Elon Musk's plans for an Interplanetary Transport System is exciting, but nonetheless is a challenging prospect with many questions left unanswered and many gaps to fill. He highlights four major challenges that SpaceX and other entities will face going to Mars:

1. Full Reusability;
2. Refilling in Orbit;
3. Propellant production on Mars;
4. Right propellant

Musk's plan for colonizing Mars includes the development of an intricate and robust transport system with the ability to carry over 100 passengers on a vehicle that has forty-two engines. SpaceX plans to use a fully reusable vehicle that runs on cheaper fuel (but difficult to find). Current cost estimates to send a person to Mars runs approximately $10 billion per person, but the ultimate goal is to reduce that price to about $100,000 per seat. But even with this lower ticket price, a trip to Mars is still not feasible for the mass market they are trying to reach.

What everyone clearly agrees on is increasing access to space for anyone that is interested, while reducing the costs, and significantly cutting the gap between those who want to go and those who can afford to go. This, in itself, poses one of the greatest challenges. But many of these companies have revealed their plans in smaller, short-term proposals with a more general long-term vision in mind. Musk's ambitious 100-year plan is perhaps an attempt to take the lead on discussions for the colonization of Mars.

We will be forever balancing our dreams and visions for exploration with the harsh reality of risk and budgetary constraints. And while Musk's presentation was inspirational, there is an unfortunate reality that companies like SpaceX, among others, will need to face.

EVALUATING THE AUTHOR'S ARGUMENTS:

In this viewpoint, Mia Brown notes some of the challenges to colonizing Mars. From the information given, does it appear that SpaceX will be able to overcome those challenges?

Exploring Space Makes Life on Earth Better

"As a direct result of the innovations, inventions, and discoveries that have enabled us to explore space, our daily lives on Earth have changed profoundly."

Space Foundation

In the following viewpoint, the Space Foundation argues the benefits to space exploration. The authors contend that many important technological advances have come from the space program. Not all of these technologies came directly from space exploration in a finished form. Yet often NASA and the companies, universities, and laboratories working with it were involved at some stage. When this is considered, the cost of space exploration seems to be an excellent investment. The Space Foundation is a nonprofit organization that promotes the global space industry.

AS YOU READ, CONSIDER THE FOLLOWING QUESTIONS:
1. What are some common consumer goods that have come out of the program?
2. How are satellites important to daily life, according to the article?
3. Why is it hard to say exactly how much money space exploration contributes to the economy?

"The Case for Space Exploration," Space Foundation. Reprinted by permission.

Satellite technology has improved our lives on Earth immeasurably. In fact, many of the things we have learned to rely on originated with the space program.

Space exploration requires experts in many different areas to work together to develop entirely new capabilities that operate reliably in a remote and hostile environment. Few other endeavors combine this interdisciplinary focus with the need to achieve not simply concepts or demonstrations, but also functional end-state results. No other endeavor addresses the same challenges as space exploration. Many of the capabilities and technologies we have developed through space exploration probably would not have been developed in its absence, even with the same level of investment.

Goods and services enabled through the use and exploration of space permeate our economy. Massive industries, with annual revenues of hundreds of billions to trillions of dollars, rely on space systems to provide key capabilities. From television to cell phones, from maps to weather forecasts, fundamental aspects of American life rely on an infrastructure of in-space systems in place today. Many others—personal computers, compact discs, and cordless tools, among countless examples—derive in part from past investments in space technology.

Moreover, the impact of investment in space exploration extends far beyond the United States and the small number of other space-faring nations. Space capabilities shape life around the world.

Space Infrastructure

The global space economy is built on a space infrastructure consisting of manufacturers, service providers, and technologists in industry and government who deploy and operate launch vehicles, satellites, and space platforms such as the International Space Station. The cost of this space infrastructure is borne by commercial firms that sell satellite services; governments in many countries that use satellites to provide long-distance telephone, television, and Internet to their citizens; and the national space agencies (mainly those of the United States, Europe, Russia, Ukraine, China, Japan, and a few others). The cost of space infrastructure—launchers, in-space systems and supporting ground operations, human activity in space, and the knowledge and technology base that supports the infrastructure—is about $60 billion each year. That includes every cent of NASA's budget, the budgets of all other international space agencies, the cost of military space activities, and nearly $13 billion of commercial expenditure on manufacturing and deploying commercial satellites and launchers.

This investment enables not only space exploration, with its extraordinarily rich legacy of science, inspiration, and human achievement, but also economic activity many times larger. Our spending on space delivers vast and growing improvements in quality of life, safety, security, health, and education in the United States and around the world.

Goods and Services That Use the Space Infrastructure

Goods and services relying on space infrastructure generate hundreds of billions of dollars in direct revenue, and in doing so enable important industries that are much larger. In fact, a defining feature of many space-related goods and services is that their cost is tiny compared to the convenience, efficiency, information, and other benefits they yield.

For example, most people would list direct-to-home television and satellite radio as space-related industries, and indeed, these services generate more than $50 billion in revenue each year, and provide access to television and radio to many new subscribers. Much more sweeping, however, is the use of space by broadcast and cable television. Broadcast and cable television providers rely on satellites to distribute nearly all content to cable head ends and broadcast affiliates and to transmit new feeds from location to studio.

Satellites also enable truly global Internet service. Satellites are not the primary mode of Internet communications, but they extend Internet content and access in ways that current terrestrial networks simply cannot accommodate. Satellites provide intercontinental capacity to augment fiber optic cable networks that underserve certain pathways, such as those between South America and Asia, or along many parts of the African coastline. Satellite connections have also allowed many Internet users to receive broadband service without waiting the years that it is taking in some areas to build high-speed landline connections.

Long-distance telephone service via satellite was the earliest widespread space application and delivered instant telephone access between United States and many other countries. Today, nearly all long-distance calls leaving the United States travel on fiber optic cables, but many nations that are not connected to cable networks due to expense or geography still depend on satellites.

Leasing satellite capacity for television, telephone, and Internet backbone around the world generates about $10 billion each year directly to satellite owners and operators. However, the true economic power of these applications of satellites is in the worldwide access to communication services, education, news, information, and entertainment provided to billions of people. In fact, they exemplify what is perhaps the most powerful statement to be made about space exploration and the global economy—that the concept of a global economy is difficult to imagine in the absence of global communications, and global communications exist because of space capabilities.

Satellite navigation is another excellent example of the disproportionate benefits delivered by space goods and services. This global industry exists solely due to a service provided free to the world by the United States through the Global Positioning System (GPS) constellation of satellites. GPS satellite signals allow users on land, on the sea, and in the air with inexpensive GPS devices to determine their position and, aided by computer maps (most of which were developed in part using other satellite capabilities such as remote sensing), plot a course to their destination. GPS navigation has been so successful and valuable that that the European Space Agency is investing billions of dollars to develop its own GPS satellite constellation, Gallileo. GPS signals also provide precision timing for financial and cell phone networks.

Consumers increasingly rely on products and services such as On-Star, the General Motors GPS system that provides drivers with directions via the cell phone network and DVD navigation systems that integrate maps with automated voice directions. Industrial applications include trucking, aviation, and maritime services. Manufacture of GPS navigation units and direct purchase of associated value-added products and services generates about $18 billion in revenue, with high annual growth. These dollar values do not, of course, reflect the time saved, improved safety, and reduced costs that users of these systems have realized.

There are many other examples. Almost $2 billion is paid each year for satellite images and basic processing, but analysis and use of the information they generate is a fundamental part of many massive industries. Satellite imaging is increasingly familiar to all of us, as we see satellite pictures of the Earth used for mapping, surveying, crop monitoring, assessing environmental health, evaluating traffic and land use impacts, military reconnaissance, and many other applications. As population has risen, demands on farmers, land developers, and transportation infrastructure to obtain the best possible use of property have risen, and the value of these geographic information programs and services is multiplied to the extent that they meet these needs.

Thousands of gas stations use inexpensive small satellite dishes (very small aperture terminals, or VSATS) to connect to dedicated communication networks that let them nearly instantly process credit cards at their outdoor pumps. Just about every adult in the United States has relished the convenience of these speedy transactions. Internet cafes in Europe connect to the Internet, chains receive data for "digital signage" in individual stores, and remote island regions establish telephone service using VSATS.

In summary, the quality-of-life benefits yielded by space goods and services are sweeping and significant, with tremendous value in time saved, injuries and casualties avoided, education enabled, and efficiencies realized.

Space Technologies Transforming Daily Life

Perhaps even more valuable than the goods and services that use space infrastructure are those that use technologies developed as part of space exploration. The impacts of these technologies are so ubiquitous that it is difficult to imagine life without them.

Just a few award-winning examples are illustrated here. However, even a complete list of specific spinoffs would understate the impact of work conducted by NASA and the companies, universities, and laboratories it has funded. Space exploration technology has had a profound impact on the full range of industries that define modern life, including computing, telecommunications, medicine, aviation, and many others.

For example, computing and digital data storage media such as compact discs rely on error correction code technologies pioneered by NASA to compensate for "noisy" signals from low power transmitters used to save weight and space in early launches.

Television and telephone signals are compressed so massive amounts of information can be carried using limited bandwidth and small devices, drawing on decades of research on wireless communications in space. Surgeons and doctors rely on imaging technologies such as magnetic resonance imaging, precision miniaturized surgical instruments, laser devices, and advanced materials that have their origins with astronauts and space hardware. Flight simulation systems, advanced avionics, automated instrumentation, and other features of commercial airliners derive from NASA aeronautics and aerospace research.

The pathways taken by these capabilities often meander in and out of NASA's programs, as technologies are transferred from NASA field centers and contractors to operational space programs. They are reused, adapted, and enhanced by other organizations in industry, the military, or academia, and then sometimes reinserted in NASA's technology stream or perhaps combined with commercial research and development projects. While these complex interactions make it more difficult to map the precise pedigree of space-derived products or to compile a complete listing, the interplay among disciplines, organizations, and users makes the legacy of space exploration technology richer.

What the Future Holds

We can state with certainty that the unique problems and powerful problem-solving environment of space exploration will continue to enrich our economy and our lives. While we can make some guesses about what new capabilities, goods and services will result (environmentally useful water and agriculture techniques, new sources of power for tiny mobile devices, ultra-high precision products manufactured in space, or even public space travel on short suborbital flights), we can state with equal certainty that we don't know for sure. The process of space exploration is that of conquering the unknown, and its true economic value lies in the power of transformation inherent in that very uncertainty.

Facts About Commercial Space Exploration

Editor's note: These facts can be used in reports to add credibility when making important points or claims.

Where Is Space?

- The Earth has a layer of gases surrounding the planet and held in place by gravity. This is the atmosphere.
- Most people live no more than eight kilometers (five miles) above sea level. Above that, the lack of oxygen makes it difficult to breathe.
- Mount Everest, the highest mountain on Earth, reaches about 8848 meters (29,029 feet, 5.5 miles).
- Commercial airplanes often fly at 10.5 kilometers (35,000 feet, 6.6 miles).
- The Karman line is the boundary between the Earth's atmosphere and outer space. It is defined as 100 km (62 miles) above sea level. Around this point, the atmosphere becomes too thin to support normal flight. A plane can no longer achieve any lift. A rocket or something similar must provide enough thrust to leave the Earth's orbit.
- A sub-orbital spaceflight is one that does not achieve orbital velocity. Therefore it does not stay in orbit around Earth. Instead it reenters the atmosphere and falls back to Earth within a few minutes. An engine would have to reach a very high velocity to maintain orbit. A person flying to 100 km altitude would have about three minutes of spaceflight before leaving orbit.
- An orbital spaceflight is one where the spacecraft can remain in space for at least one orbit. To do this without propulsion requires a height of approximately 150 km (90 miles).
- At an altitude of 10,000 km (6200 miles) above the Earth's surface, the absolute vacuum of space begins. At this point the Earth's atmosphere has completely ended.

How Far Have We Traveled?

- The International Space Station (ISS) orbits the Earth at 408 kilometers (254 miles).
- The moon orbits the Earth in an elliptical formation. At its closest, it is 363,104 km (225,623 miles) from Earth. At its farthest, it is 405,696 km (252,088 miles) from Earth. On average, the distance from Earth to the moon is about 384,400 km (238,855 miles). Twelve people have walked on the moon, all Americans.
- In 1970, the *Apollo 13* crew traveled farther from Earth than any humans before or since. When they traveled around the far side of the moon, they were 400,171 km (248,655 miles) away from the Earth's surface.

How Far Is Mars?

- The distance between Earth and Mars changes as the two planets travel around the sun. At their closest recorded approach, they were 56 million kilometers (34.8 million miles) apart. The average distance between Earth and Mars is 225 million km (140 million miles).
- The fastest spacecraft ever launched from Earth was NASA's New Horizons mission. It traveled at 58,000 kilometers per hour (36,000 miles per hour). At that speed, traveling a straight line, the craft would take 162 days to get to Mars when Mars is at an average distance. At the closest recorded distance between Earth and Mars, it would take 41 days.

Space Tourism

- Space tourism is space travel for pleasure or business. As of 2017, only the Russian Space Agency has taken tourists into orbital space.
- The world's first private space tourists paid over $20 million each for a ten-day visit to the International Space Station.
- Private companies working toward space tourism include SpaceX, Blue Origin, Boeing, Space Adventures, and Virgin Galactic.

Organizations to Contact

The editors have compiled the following list of organizations concerned with the issues debated in this book. The descriptions are derived from materials provided by the organizations. All have publications or information available for interested readers. The list was compiled on the date of publication of the present volume; the information provided here may change. Be aware that many organizations take several weeks or longer to respond to inquiries, so allow as much time as possible for the receipt of requested materials.

The American Association for the Advancement of Science (AAAS)
1200 New York Ave. NW
Washington DC 20005
(202) 326-6400
email: www.aaas.org/contact-AAAS
website: www.aaas.org
AAAS is an American international non-profit organization. Its goals are to "advance science, engineering, and innovation throughout the world for the benefit of all people." It publishes several science journals and shares news on its website.

American Center For Space Innovation (ACSI)
email: http://centerforspaceinnovation.org/connect
website: http://centerforspaceinnovation.org
ACSI is a voice for the commercial space industry in the United States. ACSI supports American entrepreneurs, manufacturers, and educators. The website includes a blog and a news page.

Blue Origin
21218 76th Ave S
Kent, WA 98032
(253) 437-9300
email: www.blueorigin.com/interested
website: www.blueorigin.com

Blue Origin is an American aerospace manufacturer and spaceflight services. The company was set up by Amazon.com founder Jeff Bezos. The website offers news updates on the company's activities.

The National Aeronautics and Space Administration (NASA)
300 E. Street SW, Suite 5R30
Washington, DC 20546
(202) 358-0001
e-mail: www.nasa.gov/content/submit-a-question-for-nasa
website: www.nasa.gov
NASA shares updates on NASA projects, including the planned Journey to Mars and current Mars Rover activities. Educational resources include a Kids' Club and a calendar of opportunities for students. The website contact page provides options for subscribing to news releases or following NASA on social media.

The Planetary Society
(626) 793-5100
email: tps@planetary.org
website: www.planetary.org
The Planetary Society's mission is "Empowering the world's citizens to advance space science and exploration." The website features blogs, videos, and information about space missions. It also lists events, volunteer opportunities, and contests. Paid members receive special content.

Space Foundation
4425 Arrowswest Dr
Colorado Springs, CO 80907
(719) 576-8000
email: www.spacefoundation.org/contact
website: www.spacefoundation.org
This nonprofit organization's goal is to "inspire, educate, connect, and advocate on behalf of the global space community." People can visit the Space Foundation Discovery Center. The interactive destination advances science, technology, engineering, art and mathematics (STEAM) in the context of space exploration.

The Space Studies Board (SSB)
National Research Council
500 Fifth Street, NW
Washington, DC 20001
(202) 334-3477
email: ssb@nas.edu
website: http://sites.nationalacademies.org/ssb/index.htm
The Space Studies Board is part of the National Academies of Science, Engineering, and Medicine. It provides "an independent, authoritative forum for information and advice on all aspects of space science." The website offers links to a quarterly newsletter and information on projects and events.

SpaceX
Rocket Road
Hawthorne, California 90250
(310) 363-6000
email: media@spacex.com
website: www.spacex.com
SpaceX designs, manufactures and launches rockets and spacecraft. The private company was founded in 2002 to pursue new space technology. SpaceX's ultimate goal is to enable people to live on other planets.

Universe Today
email: info@universetoday.com
website: www.universetoday.com
See videos, photos, and news articles at this site for space and astronomy news. Visit the "Guide to Space" page for information on our solar system, outer space, space exploration, and much more. Stop by the "Bad Astronomy/Universe Today forum" to ask questions of astronomy enthusiasts.

Virgin Galactic
4022 E Conant St
Long Beach, California 90808-1777
(562) 384-4400
email: https://www.virgingalactic.com/contact
website: www.virgingalactic.com
This private spaceflight company is developing commercial spacecraft. It aims to provide suborbital spaceflights to tourists and launches for space science missions. The website offers press releases and information about human spaceflight. The Spaceport America campus in New Mexico is sometimes open for tours.

For Further Reading

Books

Aldrin, Buzz. *Mission to Mars: My Vision for Space Exploration*. Des Moines, IA: National Geographic, 2015. One of the first men to land on the moon shares his ideas for humanity's future in space.

David, Leonard. *Mars: Our Future on the Red Planet*. Des Moines, IA: National Geographic, 2016. A dramatization of a possible future where people learn to live on Mars.

deGrasse Tyson, Neil. *Space Chronicles: Facing the Ultimate Frontier*. New York, NY: W. W. Norton & Company, 2012. An astrophysicist shares his views on the future of space travel.

deGrasse Tyson, Neil. *StarTalk: Everything You Ever Need to Know About Space Travel, Sci-Fi, the Human Race, the Universe, and Beyond*. Des Moines, IA: National Geographic, 2016. An illustrated companion to a National Geographic Channel show about the universe.

Guthrie, Julian. *How to Make a Spaceship: A Band of Renegades, an Epic Race, and the Birth of Private Spaceflight*. New York, NY: Penguin, 2016. An account of the first civilian spacecraft to reach outer space.

Kelly, Scott. *Endurance: A Year in Space, A Lifetime of Discovery*. New York, NY: Knopf, 2017. A memoir from an astronaut who spent a year aboard the International Space Station.

Massimino, Mike. *Spaceman: An Astronaut's Unlikely Journey to Unlock the Secrets of the Universe*. New York, NY: Crown Archetype, 2016. An astronaut shares his journeys in space exploration.

Petranek, Stephen. *How We'll Live on Mars* (TED Books). New York, NY: Simon & Schuster, 2015. A journalist insists that we can and will live on Mars, and describes how it might happen.

The Editors Of Popular Science. *The Future of Space Travel: Your New Ride to Space*. Harlan, IA: Popular Science, 2017. Short, illustrated articles covering topics such as tools of exploration and the life of an astronaut.

The Space Foundation. *America's Vision: The Case for Space Exploration*. Colorado Springs, CO: The Space Foundation, 2006. Essays by experts from Neil Armstrong to Neil deGrasse Tyson share their views on the importance of space exploration. Available online through Cornell University.

Wohlforth, Charles, and Amanda R. Hendrix Ph.D. *Beyond Earth: Our Path to a New Home in the Planets*. New York, NY: Pantheon, 2016. A look at the developments that may allow for space colonization.

Zubrin, Robert. *The Case for Mars: The Plan to Settle the Red Planet and Why We Must*. New York, NY: Free Press, 2011. A space exploration authority explains how technology may allow humans to reach and live on Mars.

Periodicals and Internet Sources

Achenbach, Joel. "Which way to space?" *The Washington Post*, November 23, 2013.

Billings, Lee. "Who Will Build the World's First Commercial Space Station?" *Scientific American*, May 26, 2017.

Casanova, Sophia, and Andrew Dempster. "Ice mined on Mars could provide water for humans exploring space," The Conversation, September 14, 2017.

David, Leonard. "Will Commercial Space Travel Blast Off in 2014?" space.com, January 11, 2014.

Dubois, Chantelle. "Drones on Mars? NASA Projects May Soon Use Drones for Space Exploration," All about Circuits, November 30, 2017.

Duggins, Pat, and Laura J. Cole. "Where to Next?" *Pegasus: The Magazine of the University of Central Florida*, Summer 2016.

Fyall, Alan, and Asli Tasci. "Opinion: Space Tourism," *Pegasus: The Magazine of the University of Central Florida*, Summer 2016.

Geggel, Laura. "City-Size Lunar Lava Tube Could House Future Astronaut Residents," Live Science, October 20, 2017.

Grady, Monica. "Private companies are launching a new space race—here's what to expect," The Conversation, October 3, 2017.

Hunter, Cameron. "China and the US are both shooting for the moon—but don't call it a space race," The Conversation, November 8, 2017.

Leahy, Bart. "Space Access: The Private Investment vs. Public Funding Debate," National Space Society, May 12, 2006.

Leckie, Ann, Jason Kehe, Katie M. Palmer, Sarah Zhang, Chelsea Leu, Matt Simon, Nick Stockton, and Adam Rogers. "The 12 Greatest Challenges for Space Exploration," *Wired*, February 16, 2016.

Liebelson, Dana. "Everything you need to know about commercial space travel," *The Week*, March 29, 2013.

Locklear, Mallory. "SpaceX's Falcon Heavy launch has been pushed to next year," Engadget, November 30, 2017.

Maynard, Andrew. "Dear Elon Musk: Your dazzling Mars plan overlooks some big nontechnical hurdles," The Conversation, October 1, 2017.

Norman, Marc, and Penelope King, "Five reasons India, China and other nations plan to travel to the Moon," The Conversation, November 19, 2017.

Russian News Agency, "Russia and China ratify agreement on protecting space exploration technologies," Russian News Agency, November 29, 2017.

Sawaya, David B. "Space tourism: Is it safe?" *OECD Observer* No 242, March 2004.

Stephen Clark, Stephen. "NASA agrees to launch station supplies on reused SpaceX rocket," Spaceflight Now, November 30, 2017.

Wall, Mike, "SpaceX's Planned Giant Rocket Could Chase Down Interstellar Asteroid," *Scientific American*, November 29, 2017.

Websites

Popular Science (https://www.popsci.com). This website provides news and technology articles on many science topics, including space travel.

Science Daily (https://www.sciencedaily.com). This science news website offers free articles on many subjects, including space exploration.

Space.com (https://www.space.com). This website covers space discoveries and missions with both breaking news and historical articles.

Index

A

Albrecht, Mark, 20, 87, 90–91
Aldrin, Andy, 31, 32
Almaz, 60
Ansari X Prize, 60
Apollo 4, 16
Apollo 8, 12, 16
Apollo 11, 54
Apollo 13, 12
Armadillo Aerospace, 60
Armstrong, Neil, 8
Asteroid Redirect Mission, 18, 22

B

beamed energy propulsion, 44
Bender, Bryan, 26–32
Berger, Eric, 87–92
Bezos, Jeff, 27, 48, 52, 60
Blue Origin, 27, 29, 48, 51, 60, 94
Boddy, Jessica, 53–58
Boeing, 12, 14, 15, 29, 32, 35, 41, 85
Branson, Richard, 7, 60
Bridenstine, Jim, 28
Britt, Daniel, 65–69
Brown, Mia, 93–97
Buzz Aldrin Space Institute, 31

C

Case for Mars, The, 81
Challenger, 57
Church, George, 72

Cold War, 34, 43, 66
Columbia, 8, 57
Colwell, Joshua, 65–69
Commerce, Justice, and Science (CJS), 21, 23, 24
Commercial Orbital Transportation Services (COTS), 75, 77
Commercial Resupply Services, 35
Constellation program, 15, 22
Coopersmith, Jonathan, 40–46
cosmic radiation, 53, 54
Crew Dragon spacecraft, 12, 14, 25, 16
Crusan, Jason, 85
Cruz, Ted, 23
Culberson, John, 21
Curry, Brendan, 31

D

Dana, Charles A., 5, 90
Daniels, Mitch, 90
Davis, Jason, 11–17
Diamandis, Peter, 72
Dreier, Casey, 18–25
Durbin, Dick, 32

E

EADS Astrium, 60
Earth science, 21
European Space Agency (ESA), 84, 102

Excalibur, 60

F
Falcon Heavy rocket, 12, 14, 15, 85
Ferreira-Snyman, Anél, 59–64
"free-return" trajectory, 12

G
Gagarin, Yuri, 41
Garver, Lori, 31
Gingrich, Newt, 28–29, 48
Government Accountability Office (GAO), 14, 49–50
ground-based system (GBS), 40–41, 43–44, 45, 46

H
Haise, Fred, 12
Hall, Alexandra, 74–75
Hauck, Rick, 49
Hawking, Stephen, 48, 52
High Altitude Research Project (HARP), 44
Honda, Mike, 21
House Science Committee, 30, 89
House Space Subcommittee, 20
Hyperion, 60

I
International Astronautical Congress (IAC), 50, 94, 95
International Space Station (ISS), 7, 8, 29, 34, 35, 36, 55, 60, 83, 95, 100

J
Joint Confidence Level (JCL),

11, 14

K
Kelly, Scott, 56
Kennedy, John F., 7, 9, 54, 66, 91–92
Kennedy Space Center, 15

L
Lansdorp, Bas, 50
Lightfoot, Robert, 88
Limoli, Charles, 54
linear electromagnetic accelerator, 77
Lockheed Martin, 32, 36–37
Lovell, Jim, 12
Lunar Orbiter, 68
Lynx, 60

M
magnetic levitation/magnetic propulsion systems, 44
Mars Colonial Transporter (MCT), 85
Mars colony
  benefits of, 80–82
  challenges to, 82–83, 93–97
  cost, 88–90
  proposed missions, 84–86
  terraforming, 83–84
Mars One, 50, 83, 85
Mars Radiation Environment Experiment (MARIE), 83
McCain, John, 32
McKay, Chris, 73, 74, 83
microgravity, 56–57, 62
Mikulski, Barbara, 21

Miller, Charles, 28
Musk, Elon, 9, 16, 27, 48, 60,
  85, 93, 94, 95, 96

N
NASA Transition Authorization
  Act, 23
National Advisory Committee
  for Aeronautics, 30
National Aeronautics and Space
  Administration (NASA)
  budgetary issues, 23–25
  effect of political change on,
    18–25
  future of, 30–32
  role in revolutionizing technol-
    ogy, 40–46
  under President Trump, 27–29
National Space Council, 20
Navarro, Peter, 20
Nelson, Bill, 23

O
Orbital ATK, 35
Orion, 22–23, 84
Orion Multi-Purpose Crew
  Vehicle (MPCV), 22, 84
Outer Space Treaty, 59, 61, 62, 63

P
Pettit, Don, 51
Politico, 26, 27
private space companies/
  exploration
  benefits of, 33–37
  dangers of, 53–58
  difficulty developing rocket

technology, 41–46
privatizing low Earth orbit
  activities, 29–30
under President Trump, 26–32
probes, 8

R
Ranger, 68
Rapid-Access Small-Cargo
  Affordable Launch
  (RASCAL), 42–43
Reuthner, James, 85
Rocketplane, 60
rockets
  alternatives to, 43–46
  cost of, 41–43
Rohrabacher, Dana, 90
Rubio, Marco, 23

S
satellites, 8, 29, 30, 32, 41, 44,
  45, 77, 98, 100, 101, 102,
  103
Saturn V, 16
Scaled Composites, 60
ScienceDebate, 20
self-replicating system (SRS), 77
Shelby, Richard, 23, 32
Shepard, Alan, 7
Shi, Lina, 33–37
Shotwell, Gwynne, 15
Smith, Lamar, 89
Soviet Union, 7, 34, 66
Soyuz, 12, 35
space colonies
  feasibility of, 47–52
  lunar, 71–78

on Mars, 79–86, 87–92,
    93–97
  obstacles and solutions, 51–52
  risks of, 49–51
space debris, 8, 59, 63
space elevators, 44
space exploration
  economic benefits of, 98–105
  human, 66
  inspirational value of, 65–69
  robotic, 67–68
Space Exploration Technologies
    Corp. (SpaceX), 9, 11, 12,
    14, 15, 16, 17, 22, 27, 29,
    32, 34, 35, 60, 85, 93,
    94–96, 97
  delays to missions, 11–17
  GAO certification, 14–15
  milestones missed by, 12–14
Space Foundation, 31, 98, 105
space fungus, 56
Space Launch System (SLS),
    22–23, 84
SpaceNews, 20
Spaceport America, 60
SpaceShipOne, 60
SpaceShipTwo, 60
Space Shuttle Program, 8,
    34–35, 36
space solar power (SSP), 76
space tourism
  dangers of, 53–58
  defining, 62–63
  delays in, 11–14
  environmental impact of,
    59–64
  legal regulations, 59–64

Sputnik, 34, 41
Stuster, Jack, 55, 56
Super High Altitude Research
    Project (SHARP), 44
Surveyor, 68
Swigert, John, 12

T
Technology Readiness Level
    (TRL), 45
Tenner, Edward, 47–52
Thiel, Peter, 27–28
Trump, Donald J., 18, 19, 20,
    21, 22, 23, 24, 26, 27, 28,
    29, 30, 31

U
United Launch Alliance, 31, 94

V
Virgin Galactic, 7, 8, 34, 36, 42,
    60, 61, 94, 95

W
Walker, Robert, 20, 27, 30
Weir, Andy, 57, 58
Whigo, Dennis, 76
Williams, Matt, 71–78, 79–86
World War II, 34, 43
Worley, Lauren, 88

X
XCOR Aerospace, 60
X Prize Foundation, 72, 74

Z
Zubrin, Robert, 81, 83

Picture Credits

Cover NASA/Getty Images, pp. 10, 67 NASA; p. 13 Bruce Weaver/ AFP/Getty Images; p. 19 Mark Wilson/Getty Images; p. 28 Getty Images; p. 35 PR images/Alamy Stock Photo; p. 39 iurii/Sutterstock. com; p. 42 3DSculptor/iStock/Thinkstock; p. 49 NASA/JPL/Cornell; p. 55 Castleski/Shutterstock.com; p. 61 Chris Butler/Science Photo Library/Getty Images; p. 70 NASA/JPL-Caltech/STScI; p. 72 Mark Stevenson/UIG/Getty Images; p. 81 Steven Hobbs/Stocktrek Images/Getty Images; p. 89 NASA/JPL/USGS; p. 94 Bloomberg/ Getty Images; p. 99 3Dsculptor/Shutterstock.com.